Group Homes for Mentally Handicapped People

Nigel Malin

LONDON: HER MAJESTY'S STATIONERY OFFICE

© *Crown copyright 1983*

First published 1983

ISBN 0 11 320841 3   2·2·84

Any views expressed in this report
are those of the author and do not
necessarily reflect those of the
Department of Health and Social Security

All names used in this report are fictitious

Acknowledgements

I wish to acknowledge the help and support of several people involved with the production of this material. Those associated with the research study need primary acknowledgement: the residents of the group homes and departmental workers — Alastair Berkeley, Pippa Mottram, Graham Sayers, Madge Garrity and others from the Family and Community Services Department, Sheffield. I wish to acknowledge Michael Bayley and Alastair Heron from the University of Sheffield for their help and to Sue Convery for typing the manuscript.

NAM
November 1982

Contents

CHAPTER 1

Current Perspectives

This book is concerned with examining issues related to group home* care for mentally handicapped people. The body of the book constitutes the findings of a large-scale research study conducted within the Sheffield area. The present chapter however is concerned with introducing key topics using a national information base: reports on local plans and strategies and many personal sources of information. It begins with specific relevant policy statements, followed by a synthesis of the issues which poses questions rather than provides statements of advice. The subject is a controversial one and the arguments raised are manifold. Present DHSS policy towards care of the mentally handicapped is stated amply in both the 1971 White Paper 'Better Services for the Mentally Handicapped' Cmmd 4683, in the 1980 review of progress since 1971, 'Mental Handicap: Progress, Problems and Priorities' and the Green Paper 'Care in the Community' (1981). The principles governing the latter are as follows:

1.1 Most people who need long term care can and should be looked after in the community. This is what most of them want for themselves and what those responsible for their care believe to be best.

1.2 There are many people in hospital who would not need to be there if appropriate community services were available. But the legal, administrative and financial framework within which health and local authorities operate presents obstacles to their transfer.'

The document proceeds to state that '. . . more could be done if resources of money and manpower were available. . . . Such services require the cooperation of neighbourhood and voluntary support, primary health care services and personal social services. . . . . (2.1) . . . . . More serious problems arise in transferring resources to enable social service depart-ments. . . . . to take responsibility for people at present in hospitals. . . . . . Increased expenditure over the last decade or so has enabled social services departments to expand their activities considerably, and joint finance has further increased the resources available to both the statutory

---

* In this study a group home refers to a residential unit consisting of a small number of people living together in an ordinary house with minimal and non residential staff support.

and voluntary services and has stimulated joint planning. However, more social services provision is needed......to provide for those being cared for in hospitals who might be better cared for in the community.' (2.2.)

It is relevant to state that 'about 15,000 mentally handicapped people at present in hospital — about one third of the total number — could be discharged immediately if appropriate services in the community were available. Their needs for support are unlikely to change and once discharged to social services care they would probably not have to return to hospital.' (3.1) '.....(T)he annual cost to the NHS of caring for 15,000 mentally handicapped hospital patients was about £90 million in 1979/80, or an average £6000 per patient.....' (3.4.)

The 1980 review concluded that the 1971 White Paper target for hospital places for children was excessive and that it was likely that the White Paper over-estimated the number of places for adults which will eventually be required. Regarding the extension of residential care in the community through the use of ordinary housing accommodation, the review said:

'Further work is required on whether greater use can be made of group homes, satellite housing, lodgings or ordinary housing.' (2.53 iv.)

In recent years there has been much effort to express a *philosophy of care* for the mentally handicapped in the preambles of working documents and strategic formulae set to provide services for given areas, eg Northumberland, Sheffield. Some mention must be made of the Kings Fund incentive to organise a working group in 1978 with the intention of developing policies for residential care within the community. Its principles are now well known:

Mentally handicapped people have the same human value as anyone else.
Mentally handicapped people have a right and a need to live like others in the community.
Services must recognise the individuality of mentally handicapped people.

There has been little research in the area of group home care, although reports exist covering details on local schemes and initiatives eg Craft and Evans (1970), Johnson (1975), Chant (1977), Gardham *et al* (1977).* The study of the 'Cherries' group home (Race and Race, 1978) suggests that residents showed some improvements in independence skills but that personality factors were of overriding importance in enabling the home to function. In relation to community attitudes Grunewald and Thor (1978) reported that having too large a group in one unit led to public opposition to the group homes in general. Baker *et al* (1977) have pointed to the

---

* In 1983 (after the research described in this book was completed) the Department of the Environment published a report of a research study of housing provisions in England and Wales 'Housing for mentally ill and mentally handicapped people' by Jane Ritchie and Jill Keegan which provided a profile of the amount and type of housing (including group homes provided by local housing authorities, housing associations and voluntary organisations) and assessed the different forms of housing with particular reference to their development, organisation and support.

problem of staff in small units becoming isolated and institutionalised whilst the residents became integrated and de-institutionalised. There is also the problem of job mobility and promotion prospects unless the unit is part of a larger service scheme.

It would appear from current data that the main issues in a developmental context are as follows in no order of priority:

A. *Sources of housing and management*

There are three main ways of obtaining housing for group home purposes. These are through arrangements with government-sponsored housing associations, through government joint financing initiatives and through liaison with a local authority housing department. In the case of the first it is clear that much housing for mentally handicapped people is provided by housing associations. Provision of group homes for the mentally handicapped by housing associations funded through the Housing corporation has to be in accordance with:

1. The Shared Housing Supplement to the Schemework Procedure Guide.
2. The Design and Contract Criteria for Shared Housing.
3. The Cost Criteria for Shared Housing Schemes (Shared Housing Total Indicative costs).
4. HAG Eligibility Rules.

The government ensures that the Housing Corporation sets aside funds for several special groups, including mentally handicapped people, who need help in obtaining access to suitable housing.

The DOE identified housing projects for those with special needs as a priority for grant aid in Circular 170/74. They stated that groups with special needs included the elderly, the disabled, single people or other groups with special housing problems, where there is a shortage of satisfactory accommodation. The DOE in consultation with the Housing Corporation and the National Federation of Housing Associations arrives at an Approved Development Programme (ADP) for each year. This includes an apportionment of the funds available for new fair rent schemes between:

1. housing for the elderly;
2. shared housing;
3. other needs.

Shared housing projects with a warden get different allowances which reflect the cost of employing a warden. Higher management allowances are meant to cover the extra cost of managing a tenant with special needs. They are not directly related to the sort of building or the adaptations required. Very ordinary houses can get higher management allowances for a number of reasons — Paragraph 4.8 of Appendix B of DOE Circular 103/77 identify these. There is money available from the

3

Housing Corporation for housing association schemes for disabled people; and joint funding and the proposals in the Green Paper extend financing arrangements to enable long-stay hospital residents to return to the community. A Housing Corporation Practice Circular (14/81) dated July 1981 states, 'In order to receive approval to a shared housing project, a standard appraisal of the scheme must demonstrate that the project is eligible to receive housing association grant (HAG), that the anticipated level of hostel deficit grant (HDG) if any, is reasonable, that the project conforms to the relevant cost and standards criteria, that a satisfactory source of "topping up" finance has been obtained, that the proposed management arrangements are acceptable and that the planning position in relation to the project is satisfactory.'*

A scheme is considered eligible for a housing association grant where the aim and intention is *either* to provide permanent accommodation *or* to equip people with the resources and skills to live in permanent accommodation unless the project falls into one of the following categories: a mental nursing home within the meaning of the Nursing Homes Act 1975, a voluntary home within the meaning of the child Care Act 1980, which is intended for children under the age of 16, where the aim of the project to fulfil a statutory obligation other than under housing legislation, where staff are employed on the project to provide medical treatment eg drug or alcohol treatment, or where residents have another fixed place of abode while occupying the project. A project which is eligible for a housing association grant will normally have maximum ratios of staff to residents and of excess management costs to management allowance of $1:2\frac{1}{2}$ and $5:1$ respectively and that the Corporation will require evidence that exceptional circumstances apply to the project if either of these ratios is exceeded.†

The most famous record of the use of housing association grants for this purpose is the Camden project (Heginbotham, 1981). The author states that it is important to have the potential property assessed as a 'shared dwelling' rather than a hostel and therefore it will qualify for normal housing assocation grants.‡ A strenuous process began in this instance involving initial discussions between the Camden housing association and Housing Corporation to gain the blessing for grant-aid. The outcome was the setting up of a steering group of carers who organised a management agreement with the housing association which covered all aspects of management, maintenance and financial costs etc. The group home was a shared residence with 'able tenants' and the stipulation was that such tenants should provide minimal care — for

---

* This has now been updated in the Housing Corporation's 'Shared Housing Supplement to the Schemework procedure Guide' 1983.
† See the Department of Environment's Housing Association Grant Manual, November 1979.
‡ It is recognised that this is no longer necessary. Hostels and Shared Houses are now treated on the same basis.

further discussion on co-residence issues, refer to the 'Derbyshire experiment' (Malin, 1982). It was reported that Camden Mencap became the tenant and sublet to residents on the grounds that rents would work out lower. In addition rates would be halved as Mencap is a registered charity. Since opening, however, the residents have obtained jobs at £60–£70 per week. A lease was agreed upon rather than a management agreement as Mencap did not see itself as an extension of the housing association. The lease was for three years on a renewable basis with a three month 'get out' clause either way, which is hoped will never have to be used. A long period ensued whilst the tenancy agreement and letters of agreement suggested by lawyers to cover the specific situation were drafted. London Borough of Camden was satisfied but the Department of Environment required approval from the Housing Corporation. Both the Department of Environment and the Housing Corporation were unhappy about giving approval to the indirect method of granting tenancy to disabled residents yet they succumbed ultimately following considerable lobbying and pressure.

[The Housing Act (1974) stipulates that grants can only be paid to a housing association registered with the Housing Corporation. The accommodation must therefore be provided and managed by the housing association. This means that housing associations are required to have a management agreement with a voluntary association provided that the responsible steering group agrees to secure rent payments and take organisational control. (Reference: Shared Housing Supplement to the Schemework Procedure Guide.)] All the residents were graded as householders by the DHSS and therefore qualified for fullscale benefit plus an amount for rent and rates. The main furniture for the group home was acquired through donations and gifts (John Strand Furnishing Company, MIND grant of £400 bought a washing machine, tumble drier and extras).* A management committee of the steering group looked after the home from then on. Subsequently a joint group homes management committee was set up to run the five Camden houses and general issues are dealt with there.

Money is earmarked by the Housing Corporation for 'shared housing' projects *not* special needs. However, the provision of housing for people with special needs is a priority of the Housing Corporation. Proper arrangements through a management agreement ensure proper management and accountability. The Camden experience showed however, that a direct lease can be made to tenants through a housing association

---

* It is recognised that shared housing projects are eligible to claim the 'furniture allowance'.

provided assurances of support to guarantee rent are made.* L'Arche, a voluntary organisation, has experience of a housing association arrangement, yet it argues strongly that cooperation with a 'caring group' is to the advantage of both sides. The main agency, in this case L'Arche, has to secure running costs, for such as staffing, in relation to the requirements of care to satisfy the local authority or health authority or whoever is responsible for the basic upkeep of the home whilst the 'caring group' entering into agreement needs to ensure rent payment which is the crucial concern regarding arrangements with a housing authority. Brent Social Services Department had a similar arrangement with the formation of a steering group representing Brent Mencap, Brent social services department and Brent housing association for the purposes of obtaining a single property for four residents. It is not known, however, whether this initiative has been extended for future purposes — altogether, a grant of £60,000 was acquired for purchase and conversion. In addition the Mencap Homes Foundation will seek and accept properties and gifts from any source and will use these to provide homes for mentally handicapped people. The properties are transferred into the name of Mencap Homeway Ltd which is responsible for managing them. A main aim is to work in close cooperation with local authorities and health authorities. Groups of homes will be supervised by an area management committee and will operate on a self-financing basis. The New Era housing association, so-named, is closely linked with Mencap. It will be used up to the limit to which Housing Corporation funds are made available. The Foundation intends to cooperate with housing associations and seek ways of creating homes by applying for joint funding or urban aid grants. Foundation homes, having been set up, are self-financing in the sense that their revenue income and expenditure must balance. Those residents who are earning a living are expected to make a contribution towards the cost of maintaining their home and providing food. Similar contributions will be expected from residents, who receive supplementary benefit or local authority or health authority sponsorship. As it is essential that homes are self-financing, application for deficit of payments are sought from local authorities who are represented on the committees responsible for running the homes. It is suggested (Mencap, 1982) that local Mencap societies should be able to raise money towards improvements and amenities within the homes. There will be also homes where some form of permanent endowment has been provided as a result

---

* A lease can only be granted to a voluntary organisation where:
1. both parties to the lease are registered housing associations, and the lease from the developing to the managing association enables the latter to assume full responsibility for the project OR
2. the lease is to an organisation other than a registered housing association and it is drawn up in conjunction with a separate management agreement which is referred to under covenant in the main body of the lease. The lease can then stipulate that a breach of the management agreement constitutes grounds for terminating the lease. (See Section 1.4 para 3c of the Shared Housing Supplement to the Schemework Procedure Guide). There is no requirement to guarantee rents.

6

of the creation of a private trust (in the transfer of property to the mentally handicapped relative) and some agreement with parents may also provide funds to supplement income. Acquisition of properties involves expenses such as stamp duties, legal fees and land requisition fees, and capital transfer tax may be incurred. An area management committee will be responsible for each group of homes managed by the Foundation. The members of these committees are appointed and if necessary discharged by the Foundation. The membership will entail a chairman, vicechairman, representatives of the local social services department, a representative of the district health authority, representatives from local Mencap societies, a nominee of the Foundation, Director of Mencap regional services and additional coopted members.

The method of joint financing has enormous potential for the acquisition of properties to be used for group home purposes as its aims are directed towards the care of people being moved from hospital to the community. The Green Paper 'Care in the Community' (1981) states that in 1976 the DHSS introduced joint financing to enable NHS funds to be used for collaborative projects primarily in the personal social services field for the better care of patients. As the scheme has developed its flexibility has increased.* All capital and revenue costs for a scheme are met for up to three years. Revenue costs can be made from NHS funds on a reducing scale (tapering) for up to a further four years, or longer with approval of the Secretary of State. It is, however, a *fundamental principle* of the scheme that responsibility for the revenue consequences of community provision should in due course pass to the social services department or a voluntary organisation. Joint financing has obvious benefits but local authorities have been cautious in taking up suggestions due to several inherent limitations of the scheme:

a.any project entails commitment to future revenue costs, when resources available to social service departments in the future are uncertain;

b.it provides no guaranteed source of funds for major extensions of personal social services; decisions are made on individual schemes;

c.it does not extend to a local authority's housing and education responsibilities although these may be involved when people are transferred from hospital to the care of a social services department;

d.it may limit the freedom of councillors to decide on long-term priorities in planning services.

Some organisations argue that joint financing is a better method where there is a real interest all round in the project concerned. If social services

---

* Current provision for joint finance is set out in the Health Social Services and Social Security Adjudications Act 1983; 100% joint finance is now available in some circumstances for 10 years with a further tapering over 5 years.

arrange or provide accommodation the residents are likely to be eligible for higher social security benefits, enough to provide an adequate basis for ordinary family budgeting. It is then possible to arrange a safeguard with the social services department in the form of a 'topping-up' which makes good any short-fall per annum.

As a further alternative, houses may be provided for group home purposes directly from local authorities either through making clients normal members of the local authority housing waiting list or through special arrangements with the social services department. A good example is the recent Sheffield experience where a development section has been set up since January 1980 which has taken a major responsibility for liaison with the housing department to acquire houses for set purposes. In practice it has advertised a brief within the department for sponsorship of specific projects. Therefore the onus has been placed on residential, social and advisory workers to put forward a case for a group home for a selected group. Certain experiences are worth quoting in view of the attitudes they present of professional workers being 'caught up' in this channel of events. On the one hand there are clear prejudices against such centralised developments as they are seen to discourage independent initiatives. The negotiation for house possession is left in the hands of administrators, leaving the residential workers feeling resentful of their inadequate involvement. Yet successes are evident where a good relationship has arisen between relevant officers: those from the housing department, the staff from the hostel, social services advisory staff, social workers and divisional officers. Such an example has proved a 'tricky alliance' owing its success largely to the initiative of the hostel principal. Some hostel principals have refused to participate in this scheme to obtain a group home or have become disillusioned by it — a conflict over the right to manage the scheme and to choose support staff. The overall effect of this has been unfortunate judged in the light of its expected outcome. The social services department itself must accept blame for its failure to sensitise itself to the developing needs of mentally handicapped people requiring group home accommodation throughout the area and the various interests of professionals serving them in the hostels and hospitals.

There are further warnings however relating to the acquisition and planning of housing for this purpose. Centre on Environment for the Handicapped (CEH) writes informatively on relevant design criteria:

Ordinary houses: mentally handicapped peole need ordinary houses, but it is not possible to get revenue support from the Housing Corporation, for example, for hostels under six places without special adaptation, yet if social services is prepared to provide a team of peripatetic care staff supporting mentally handicapped people living in small houses and flats dotted around, then local authority or housing authority property can be used without special adaptation.

Fire precautions: only needed for larger groups; the fire officer will advise. Fully-wired alarm systems are not needed for small houses but may be recommended once a group gets more than seven or eight. Need to consider means of escape if the house is for more than five or six residents.

Planning permission: this will not be required for small houses and flats for mentally handicapped people. They are just as much local residents as anyone else. Only when the project size increases may planning permission be necessary. Permission should not normally be required for group homes where the house is 'ordinary' unless change of use is needed from some other previous function. It is needed almost certainly if the number of residents exceeds six or seven, especially if other services are provided. When planning permission is required then the local authority will notify immediate neighbours to seek their views. If permission is going to be needed it is probably best to have a quiet word with some of the neighbours before they receive the notification.

Wardens/careworkers: sometimes planning permission is only granted if there is to be 24-hour cover and that can mean a living-in staff member. This has disadvantages, firstly that the warden is never away from work and this can be a considerable strain, secondly, there is a tendency to attract people to the job because of the accommodation rather than the job itself. To be a hostel and claim hostel deficit grant towards any deficit on the running costs, at least 6 bedspaces must be provided, but several houses each with less than 6 bedspaces may be run as a dispersed hostel with a peripatetic warden, provided that there are at least 6 bedspaces in total. All forms of shared housing are treated in the same way for Housing Association Grant purposes.

Shared housing (wear and tear on furniture and fittings): in any shared housing there is a tendency for people to be less considerate towards furniture, decorations and fittings. Even where the residents are involved in redecorating, experience has shown that individuals do not think about redecorating when they stick up posters or play darts. It is important to bear in mind: (i) cost of replacement of furniture, crockery etc can be quite high. Furniture in particular does not wear as well and tends to be treated quite badly. If incontinent friends come to stay, settees can be ruined overnight. Any revenue budget needs to take into account the cost of repairs or replacements so that decent homely furniture can be provided, otherwise there is a tendency to institutionalise furniture; (ii) cost of replacing carpets is very high. Preferably good quality haircord should be provided in communal areas. Carpet can wear very fast in hallways and sitting rooms.

9

Kitchens: size is important, depending on the number of people in the house. For any one time in an evening there may be, for example, two people cooking their own meal, a care assistant teaching two people to cook, two people sitting at the table chatting to a volunteer, a social worker who has just come to see a client. Good size is needed for any group greater than five or six. Good storage cupboards are needed: individuals living semi-independently will have their own food. Avoid waste disposal units: nasty tendency to 'eat' teaspoons etc.

Bedroom size/space: needs to be adequate; need for privacy and storage space.

Bathrooms/toilets: as a rough guide, one bathroom per four people and an extra toilet — each person must have privacy and no two people should be expected to use a bathroom at the same time.

Central heating: from both a functional and management point of view central heating is important in any group living. The system is flexible; it allows bills to be paid centrally and charged weekly; it is equitable and it reduces fire risks of individual tenants having paraffin stoves etc. It is also cheaper overall.

Utility room and washing machines: a utility room with a washing machine and tumble dryer is useful because in a shared house extra space away from the kitchen will reduce overcrowding of one room. A lot of people have washers and tumblers so why not the mentally handicapped; it encourages cleanliness; it is a form of income subsidy as launderettes are very expensive; it is essential if anyone is incontinent.

Gardens: gardens can be marvellous or they can be a curse. Sometimes they are well-used (often by non-handicapped residents); occasionally they are left barren. They are a teaching resource but will often need to be started, possibly professionally, and can be expensive; need to buy garden implements.

Ramped access/wheelchair provision: wherever possible the ground floor of any house should be converted to allow wheelchair access, or at least with appropriate width doors so that other adaptations can be provided later.

Telephone: pay phones are preferable but may be broken into from time to time. If residents are physically handicapped then the phone must not be placed too high upon the wall.

Institutionalisation: try to minimise institutional effects, e.g. plastic chairs, an office of staff, shelves in hall with incontinence pads. Let residents choose their own carpet, wallpaper, curtains. If residents wish to 'do their own thing' it should be encouraged — one resident painted a wall in green gloss; not everyone's cup of tea but his choice, his room, he had to live with it. On the other hand, it is wrong to think that all mentally handicapped people want bright colours!!!; some will, some won't like the rest of us.

Burglary prevention and insurance: mentally handicapped people are often thoughtless about such issues so it is a good idea to provide special window catches and mortice locks. These may be required before insurance can be obtained. The housing association or local Mencap can insure the building, communal fittings and furniture but not the contents of individual rooms.

Locks: on residents' doors. Some have a snib on the inside and a key for the outside and can in an emergency be removed from outside with an appropriate tool.

General storage; Appliances: there may be a number (central heating, boilers, cooker, fires, fridges); these need to be regularly serviced or else they can become dangerous.

A final note: as regards individual monetary allowances, a formal arrangement showing the involvement of a 'caring agent' either through joint financing, local authority housing liaison with a social services department or through a housing association agreement has proved of benefit to residents in terms of DHSS grants, including exemption from council rate payments. Concerning the equipping of homes, experience has shown the importance of a 'caring group' or voluntary body in obtaining essential requirements. The question might be raised as to whether it is right that a 'caring group' acting on the part of the housing association or even a social services department should be in a position to 'top up' payments for rent, rates and other services if the handicapped residents fail to budget successfully. Underlining this is the further consideration of how much should the State agree to support the needs of the handicapped and to improve their quality of life.

As regards main administration, it is fair to expect, at least at the intitial stages, a formal arrangement for rent payment between a housing and caring agency. It would then be sensible for the caring agency to work towards making the client group more independent of its aid so as to enable the housing agency to deal directly with the clients. A way of progressing to this stage is for there to be a vast expansion of the use of ordinary housing involving greater liaison between the housing department and the client, with a caring agency acting as intermediary. There would then be a basis for developing direct agreements between housing agencies and mentally handicapped citizens, with the consequent furtherance of a welfare role for housing departments. The caring agency, e.g. the social services department, should correspondingly review its role towards advocacy, with the function of helping mentally handicapped people to help themselves.

11

Lastly, the issue of general costs: comparisons need to be made among units and types of unit, principally between group home and hostel or hospital care. Costs including social costs need to be balanced against benefits to clients and families. Most group home schemes insist on self-financing (Mencap, Northumberland Action Plan) insofar as residents' incomes are expected to meet respective outgoings. This does not take account of means for staff support, initial equipment or development. A clear comparison, however, might be drawn in the case of capital costs: to take Sheffield by example, in 1980 a 24-bedded purpose-built hostel was costing around £280,000 whereas a good quality semi-detached residence suitable for five people was available for purchase for £30,000. In the case of the first, the figure excludes interest payments on the capital loan. As an anecdote: at present in Sheffield a house for eight mentally hanidcapped adults is being built within the grounds of a hostel. This is for training purposes relevant to group home placement, is to cost between £65–80,000 and is due for completion by June 1983. Arguably this type of facility cannot provide proper training opportunities for "community" living as it is not actually set within an ordinary neighbourhood. In addition it is cost restrictive as better training should be possible in two ordinary houses each for four residents (say) at £30,000. Cost comparisons are urgently required in relation to staffing needs for both purpose-built and non-purpose built units.

B. *Selection of residents and relevant criteria*

In general there are no fixed criteria for determining which mentally handicapped people are suitable for group homes. This again is a subject of dispute based on notions of which residents have the greatest chance of 'success' and prejudices against handicapped people with specific disabilities. Not only is there ample evidence to suggest that the net 'for intake' has no boundaries but also there is a lack of serious argument to defend existing criteria. There are those who claim that younger residents have the greater right and others who would consider excluding people on the grounds of physical frailty, old age, or psychological disturbance. It is significant that more reference is now made to 'group harmony' factors with emphasis on personalities working as a team as being essential to survival. Insufficient priority has in the past been paid to selecting people who get on well together as opposed to their competence in self-care. Yet no wide acceptance of this as a basic prerequisite exists and questions remain dominated by the issue of "what is the right mix of residents?" and the rider "surely the multiply handicapped or mixed sexes or people of different ages or people with a history of aggressive or disturbed behaviour must be excluded?"

The position at present is that individual service agencies choose a form of assessment either employing an established method e.g. Progress Assessment Charts, Adaptive Behaviour Scale, or else devising their own which covers a range of social and self-help skills concerning academic, motor skill, perceptual and vocational areas. For example, one hostel has the following checklist: 0 = Needs Full Supervision, 1 = Needs Minimum Supervision, 2 = Needs No Supervision, to be marked as appropriate against individual items. Some practitioners, e.g Zadik (1980), have extended the range of skill areas within their checklist to obtain a full picture of the mentally handicapped person's range of abilities and behaviours. This is all very well but no amount of exhaustive data on an individual's strengths, weaknesses, handicaps, interests and otherwise will provide the necessary tool for determining eligibility to live in a group home. Two principal factors emerge: a) an individual's ability to survive in a group home depends on the amount/type of interchange he/she is to have with co-residents and b) external support may contribute substantially to the ability of the group to gell as a "freestanding unit". One might add that these two criteria apply similarly to non-handicapped people living in a group setting. This is an important factor that mentally handicapped people should be viewed similarly and seen as having the same 'problems of relating' as others for the purposes of living and sharing together.

One local authority that selects tenants from its hostels uses the following criteria: a) ability to tell the time, b) ability to use telephone, c) ability to recognise strangers, d) knowledge of public transport, e) use of money, f) do their own shopping, g) ability to prepare simple meals. This appears to be a typical 'shopping list' of items used by staff and has justification given the types of skills seen as essential requirements for community living. Standing alone, however, its deficit is that it takes no account of how individuals complement each other's needs. Surely the argument for group home living is that minimal support is provided to a small group of mentally handicapped individuals geared towards their needs as a group. Account should be taken of what they are able to give and take from one another as a group and that any external support offered should relate to the outcome of these internal relationships. This conclusion provides a useful lead-in to the problem of 'what type of training, preparation, help and support is needed' for mentally handicapped people to live together. It raises the issue of whether it is at all practicable to devise a checklist prescribing individual living skills relevant for group home accommodation. Compatibility is very relevant to decisions concerning an individual's lack of suitability for a group home and where he might be placed thereafter. Should his preferences for living with individuals A, B and C be taken into consideration? — conversely should an established group have the final say for choosing a co-resident? These questions of 'rights' are very important in the context of evaluation when notions of 'needs', 'justice' and 'effectiveness' are considered. If the goal in community services for the handicapped is normalisation then surely the right to choose where one lives must be relevant.

C. *Preparatory training and staff support*

The essential question is 'What is the right type of training to give to residents and what should constitute staff support?' Camden social services department had the experience of dealing with community service volunteers (CSV) for the purposes of a shared living scheme: 'We found a young couple who were squatting and wanted a home and were eager to join the project. They had a male friend who was a student and was at home during the day and hence cooked; this was useful as he was able to show tenants that cooking was not simply "women's work". The able tenants do not have formal responsibilities to the group but the department pays them £4 per week as good neighbours and this helps to offset the work they do.' The difficulty lies in teaching residents how to do things for themselves and become a member of the community involving coping with the feeling of anxiety, insecurity and rejection following a long institutional life. Staff have anxieties as to what is the right kind of supervision for group home living. Arguments are conducted over the appropriateness of preparation: 'we are using small training areas in the hostel to prepare residents for independent living but I suspect it would be preferable to train in a group home or independent living unit from the start as transfer of training, for example, from cooking with a different cooker is not easy' (hostel principal).

Staff state aims in terms such as 'developing potential' of residents, 'making (them) as independent as possible' and 'making (their) lives like that of non-handicapped, normal people' but fail to show, in general, how they propose to achieve these aims in any systematic way. Some examples of training successes are on record but these relate to particular skill development and not to the achievement of living independent of service support. L'Arche's philosophy is that 'the most important part of care is to have a relationship with handicapped people and to allow them to reciprocate'. The idea is based on the assumption that mentally handicapped people have many gifts and that these should be properly recognised. This is supported by CMH writings: 'Individuals going to a group home learn the hard way what could have been taught earlier, e.g. dealing with bills, social security, debts. Our job is to present the handicapped person in the most positive valued way and teach our friends, neighbours and society in general that ordinary responses bring ordinary interactions. The staff's job is to help mentally handicapped people to live, have fun, share and thus learn from and teach each person.' This is a teaching concept based on development of the person where the teacher first gets to know the person and then helps to develop him in a way that is fitting to his needs. This involves a development of self-awareness on the part of the mentally handicapped person; yet requires a one-to-one relationship with a teacher.

Leicestershire County Council has appointed a group homes training officer to support and educate staff in the task of setting up group homes.

The project concerns the development of staff skills for the support of group homes on the understanding that this type of facility is to increase. One issue that has emerged concerns staff turnover and the right of residents to dictate to staff what is needed in the way of support. In one case the handicapped residents taught house traditions to new support staff given the existence of a formal group home management body. The Kingston experience concerning the development of a group home in Barnes emphasises the importance of trained community nurses in both preparing residents for group home living and in providing subsequent support. The question of the right kind of staff has been raised: calibre and training background are the most essential points. The Sheffield experience refers to the need for both trained staff and staff already familiar with the residents prior to their move to a group home. The account of a hostel principal says it all — although the underlying need for flexibility in deciding on support and care emerges:

'Our principal assistant said what are we doing about a group home? I didn't want a home help, I wanted a satellite from here, something we can be involved in. The principal assistant was on my side but the divisional officer and fieldworkers said that group homes should be divisionally-based and the Director of Social Services agreed. We decided to try and work the the division and make it a 50/50: they employed a new social work assistant. The principal social worker said that he, the social work assistant, me and care staff should be involved in supporting residents. Yet departmental policy was that homes should be a fieldwork responsibility. We wanted a satellite however and showed our insistence on this; the principal assistant told me to contact the development section that was apparently beginning to process applications for this type of thing. The development section officer helped me to fill in the forms and began to contact housing. It was my principal assistant who pushed me in all this. The housing department had committed itself to providing a number of houses; it was about six months between contacting the development section and obtaining the property. We'd worked with the group for about one year prior to contacting the development section.'

There are disputes, in general, on a national basis as to which type of staff are the most appropriate in providing support at group home level: home help, social worker, social work assistant, community nurse, hospital ancillaries, a social services warden, volunteers or non-handicapped co-residents — there are no clear-cut answers, only experience will show the way and different authorities have a story to tell! The main lesson concerns the promulgation of training; experiences provide a contribution to the compilation of suitable training programmes for staff fitting this task. Yet the lessons learned do not dictate sufficiently proper training criteria: a full conceptually-based programme is required translated into specified goals and methods. 'Homemaking' (used in both the Kings Fund 'An Ordinary Life' document and Guys Health District Development Plan) as a task-base is inadequate without a strict practice code but a relevant beginning to a much-needed debate.

15

The experience of Newcastle social services department in its establishment of five group homes (up to April 1982) refers to the need for the monitoring of resident behaviour through periodic assessment and reassessment and the maintenance of individual programme plans (IPPs). The aim is normalisation 'that all mentally handicapped people will become useful and meaningful members of the community'. A letter received from a community health council member writes of the importance of ensuring that each handicapped person moved into the community has someone concerned with his or her particular wellbeing against the risk of his/her becoming a 'statistical success' but 'an unknown case' (without any protection or support). 'My experience was with a mentally handicapped man in his late 30s living at home until the death of his mother, then taken into a hostel for a short period before a council house placement with three other persons. He deteriorated quickly, not eating, became aggressive and finally was admitted to hospital with blackouts. The hostel staff supervised the house, also ATC staff; all knew of J's difficulties but who had ultimate responsibility for J's happiness and safety? I believe that there must be someone, one person with final authority for the quality of life of each handicapped adult and that that person should be close to the client not a remote psychiatric consultant.'

Camden social services policy document discusses the concept of a 'core and cluster' scheme which would entail, amongst other things, the use of keyworkers as recommended by the above. 'Keyworker' contact has been approved by the DES *Warnock Report* (1978) and by the *Strategic Plan* (1981) of services for the mentally handicapped in Sheffield. The 'core and cluster' scheme is an emulation of the ENCOR service structure employing a system of residential units within the community 'clustered' around a 'core unit' used for assessment and training purposes. The notion has been developed in a series of documents e.g. Jay Report (1979), An Ordinary Life (1980), Guys Health District Plan (1981). The last of these states that the concept is geared towards systemising residential care facilities on a geographical basis serving small communities. 'The major concern is monitoring, supervision and support of up to ten dispersed small residences in each system. It is, therefore, important that a strong management structure is built in each system with care to see that spans of control and supervision are not overlarge.' One management structure which has been shown to work elsewhere is shown opposite.

The diagram shows managerial relationships (*i.e.* it describes who appoints whom, who supervises whom, who reports to whom etc). It does not mean that the two parts are run completely separately, indeed the model requires a movement of staff and residents from the 'core' house into 'cluster' housing.

This type of system has been approved by Northumberland in its plan encompassing a series of group homes with minimal support but seen as

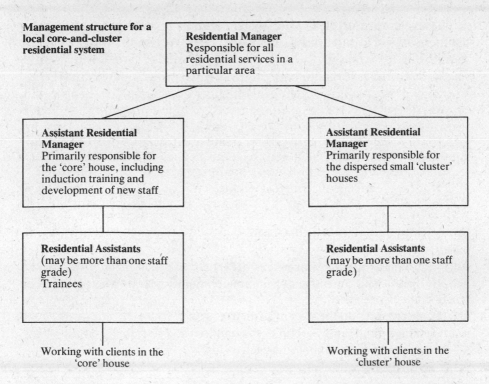

Management structure for a local core-and-cluster residential system

Residential Manager
Responsible for all residential services in a particular area

Assistant Residential Manager
Primarily responsible for the 'core' house, including induction training and development of new staff

Assistant Residential Manager
Primarily responsible for the dispersed small 'cluster' houses

Residential Assistants
(may be more than one staff grade)
Trainees

Residential Assistants
(may be more than one staff grade)

Working with clients in the 'core' house

Working with clients in the 'cluster' house

part of a full residential service to meet a defined catchment area. In general, staff are asked to help residents to live as normal a life as possible, concentrating on self-determination — allowing residents to make decisions for themselves, and to use day facilities provided by the local authority with pressure to increase open employment opportunities. The sector administrator, Prudhoe Hospital, Northumberland, is quoted as stating that 'not only must staff have the right outlook and understand clearly the objectives of normalisation but they must develop an awareness in themselves and in the mentally handicapped person that what is normal for the rest of society is normal for them (the handicapped).' A parent gives her views on staff tasks for supporting group homes in a very lucid manner — 'to enable the client to assume maximum control over his life, involving teaching (the client) skills, allowing him to use these skills, allowing him to make decisions on what, when, where and why rather than using a lifelong time-table dictated by staff convenience, needs and desires; building self-assurance in the client by actually believing in and respecting the client as a fellow person rather than an inferior; being an advocate of the client rather than of the system.' *There is thus a need for a well-educated and trained staff.*

This is a good note upon which to end the present section. The expectations of staff are high, therefore considerable resources are needed to develop this area — the most essential to a meaningful service. Much thought needs to be given to the ingredients of training courses and the system of provision. We are currently at the start of this enterprise. As a postscript, the National Development Group document on 'Improving the Quality of Services for Mentally Handicapped People' (1980) is essential reading for those concerned with the issue of staff training both in an educational and service development sense. The meaning of 'high' quality care obtains substance through examination of activities relevant to *daily life*. The following serves as an example on this issue:

'Quality of Care: Relationships between Clients and Staff

64. In what ways do the staff help to create and foster a warm and friendly atmosphere within the unit (e.g. good relationships between clients and staff, use of friendly forms of address which are also appropriate to the person's age)?

65. How does the unit encourage continuity in relationships between a client and individual members of staff (e.g. by arranging suitable times for staff to be on duty)?

66. In order to ensure that the client receives all the individual attention he needs,

66.1 how much time do members of staff spend with each client?

66.2 is there a clear statement of a minimum number of staff who should be on the unit at any one time?

67. To what extent do the staff in a children's unit

67.1 run the unit in family groupings of children and staff?

67.2 spend some time talking with each child?

67.3 play with the children?

67.4 provide 'mothering' (including physical contact between staff and children)?

67.5 tell the children stories (e.g. at bedtimes)?

68. How much time do staff spend

68.1 training the clients in activities specified in their training plans?

68.2 following up in the unit work done by the client in outside classes and sessions (e.g. at school or at an Adult Training Centre or a programme of creative, occupational, physio or speech therapy)?

69. To what extent do staff in direct contact with residents, especially those working with children, have an adequate command of English?

70. Where there are not enough staff at any given time to ensure that standards 58–68 above are adequately met, what arrangements are there to

70.1 recruit more staff?

70.2 relieve direct care staff of routine domestic jobs?

70.3 enable direct care staff to do domestic jobs related to the care and training of clients?

70.4 recruit volunteers (as appropriate)?

71. How often are regular meetings held

71.1 of staff (e.g. to discuss individual clients, clients training plans etc)?

71.2 of staff and management (e.g. to discuss policy and individual clients and to exchange information for planning)?

71.3 of staff and clients (e.g. to discuss holidays, entertainment, outings etc)?

71.4 of clients whenever appropriate?

72. Is a dying client allowed to remain in his familiar surroundings unless there are pressing reasons to move him?

73. 'When a client dies,

73.1 are the funeral arrangements normal, dignified and in accordance with any reasonable wishes that may be expressed by him and his family?

73.2 are other clients and staff informed and enabled to attend the funeral if they wish?'

The thinking on staff education is currently within this direction but without explicit guidance. 'All staff must realise that the proposed service will demand skills not necessarily available now. It will be vital that staff attend specially designed reorientation courses and make educational visits.' (Strategic Planning of Services for the Mentally Handicapped for the area embraced by the Sheffield Area Health Authority (teaching) and Sheffield Metropolitan District Council, para. 3.2., 1981).

D. *Problems of residents' adjustment:*

The main problem concerns being moved from an institutional context to one that is semi-independent and, in reality, this involves tasks of adjustment. Basically the difficulty concerns how staff provide the necessary support and strength to help someone who has been dependent for a substantial length of time in order to deal with the obvious symptoms of anxiety, insecurity and rejection that such individuals carry with them. The difficulty on the part of residents is great although we (as non-handicapped professionals) might think otherwise — that this is an inevitable part of growing up and adapting to a normal lifestyle. Present policy recommends that people requiring permanent residential care should be dealt with in the community provided that adequate support is available. Yet there may be immense problems for individuals who have been accustomed to a 'way of life' in hospital or a hostel as they find the notion of being on their own in a group home quite difficult to cope with. In contrast, information from sources such as CMH suggests that in the view of clients the biggest benefit is being granted freedom to do as they please.

A social services director states the contrast between hospital and community placement: 'In hospital they have a feeling of security and can accept the hospital regime; they have comfortable accommodation and good food. They have pocket money more than in a group home and "for free" there is hairdressing, dances, social functions and more sexual freedom, whereas in the community they cannot cope with freedom. They are expected to identify themselves with the normal population but they don't easily accept hostel or day care because of discipline and restraint. They have, in general, inadequate living skills and are unable to budget.' This comment shows the dilemma faced by professionals and is more than somewhat biased in favour of 'letting sleeping dogs lie'. However present policy is towards normalising the lives of handicapped people, bringing with it a requirement on the part of professional workers to adjust their

19

efforts accordingly. The majority of evidence supports the move of mentally handicapped people from an institution into a group home provided that adequate account is taken of helping them to learn to live as ordinary members of the community. This may be particularly difficult for adults: 'It's harder than bringing up children as you can't get them into good ways; you get them in the mid-40s and things are harder to get out of' (hospital principal).

Group homes enable people to exercise choices unlike an institution. The emphasis is again on teaching mentally handicapped people how to do things for themselves and to live independently. The problems arising relate often to the lack of training prior to discharge yet this is enormously hard within a hostel setting — residents are looked after in large numbers, staff are limited in number and are not trained towards developing the independence of residents; more importantly neither are the principals of hostels whether they be social service or health authority trained. Then there is the problem of adapting to new individuals and a new routine. This is inevitably more difficult for some residents than for others. 'It is fairly difficult to generalise about how to respond to individual problems of adjustment' (ATC manager). How do professional workers teach adults to become independent when they have led a rather childlike existence with little recognition being made of their potential abilities? Comments from parents echo how problematic this transition is:

'Some have to be returned to hospital; they have been used to things being organised for them, in the way of leisure, meals etc.'

'However well mentally handicapped people are trained in hospital, living in the community gives rise to difficulties which cannot be simulated within the hospital setting such as dealing with house repairs, consumer complaints. These difficulties could only be overcome in a hospital hostel setting by giving the patient a requisition pad and by withdrawing support to such an extent that good staff might feel that they were not caring for the patient properly.'

'There are problems if they are moved away from friends and if they are not supported by sensible occupation and leisure time activities.'

'Those who come from hospital are definitely institutionalised and have different behaviour patterns; but most mentally handicapped people suffer from a lack of belief in their ability to cope because of the low level of expectations overtly or covertly by teachers and social service personnel.'

When people are exposed to a barren environment for many years the change to community may have an adverse effect but this must be seen as an inhibitor to development rather than a lifelong imposition of handicap. Many professionals believe that it is wrong to carry out a pre-discharge training in the traditional sense within the residential setting as this does not assist in adjustment to ordinary life within the community. It is preferable instead to select a property, move people in and then begin to help by providing relevant support training. One consultant writes that the notion of mentally handicapped people having adjustment problems is 'our excuse' for not allowing them to take risks: 'Clients' anxieties are of our own making because of our incompetence.'

The conclusion is inevitable: mentally handicapped people have no more problems than any other individual who moves from a closed protective environment to an open unprotected one. The problem depends largely on the attitude of the new community: if it is accepting and helpful the mentally handicapped person will blossom, if it is negative or unaccepting the person may be worse off than being in hospital.

There are very obvious problems associated with readjustment — the use of money, maintaining good health, fire risks, using domestic appliances to name but a few. These points need to be dealt with in the teaching sense in the hope that the person will eventually develop adequate confidence to relinquish the insecurity bestowed by dependence and move towards acquiring a sense of wellbeing. At present there is a tendency for the services to prefer younger individuals who may be less institutionalised and have the greater chance to develop and realise the need to achieve change. 'There are serious adjustment problems for those who have lived in hospital since they were under 16; whereas those admitted as adults have some experience in the community which they can refer back to. Typical problems are the difficulty of feeling comfortable in a normal sized room, being able to answer their front door — very basic problems due to their lack of experience or choices available in the past. They need to accept a new set of cultural norms.' (Adviser, social services department).

'Adjustment to independent living is difficult: mending a fuse or a blown TV — a small problem to us is a big problem to them.' (Principal, social services hostel).

A big problem for mentally handicapped people living in the community is one of learning to live with each other at the same time as coping with the pressures of life that living in the community brings. 'The only way that we have found to overcome problems of adjustment is, firstly allow the group to choose themselves whom they would like to live with and secondly, by counselling in a real-life situation not an artificial one.' (ATC manager). These difficulties of moving from a relatively protected to a relatively unprotected environment are well-recognised by most professionals employed in the mental handicap services yet it is significant that there is a lack of literature-based material discussing these matters in detail. Much has been learned on general childrearing and education but this knowledge has failed to encompass that from both experiments and experiences on teaching the mentally handicapped adult how to live and survive.

E.   *Parents' views and community acceptance*

The general view of parents towards group homes is one of wariness, offering little support to professionals who see this as a sensible means of achieving care within the community. Why are parents afraid of this option? It is perhaps only natural when their experience of bringing up a mentally handicapped child is to overprotect with good intention. Why

21

do social workers and others resent parental overprotection? Because professional ethics dictate that clients need to be allowed to develop and achieve potential. Put another way, it would seem that mentally handicapped people need either to adapt to a system of being cared for or else meet the image of a specimen for development. The attitudes of parents towards group home development have not been researched in any detail. Some views nonetheless are available but these tend towards the negative. Parents are happiest if they know that their child is going to be 'properly' cared for — how many staff are on duty? How will he/she manage transport in the morning? What about sexual issues? (The fear of exploitation, particularly in the case of females, is evident and only natural). Answer: 'OK so we put her ''on the pill'''. This is not acceptable to many parents. 'Older parents find this general problem difficult — they'd prefer if I was a more matronly type, personally I don't feel I give enough time to parents to listen to their problems' (hostel principal). Many parents resent the way that professionals take over and present judgements on how care should be given. There is much support for the village-styled community where protection and compassion appear paramount or else the small hospital or hostel setting where recreational activities are provided.

'Staff would do well to listen more to parental views rather than try to impose the latest idea from training courses. For example, not all parents share the enthusiasm for integration in the community. They feel that society has not sufficiently overcome its fears and prejudices.' (Parent).

'One of our parents believes passionately that the move to small community units is wrong. Her Downs daughter is in a 100-place NHS hospital where there is a lot of voluntary help from the local community and where the opportunities for PE and social stimulus are varied: e.g. swimming twice weekly, horse riding once per week, regular outings at weekends and evenings. She believes that schemes of the NIMROD type will lead to disastrous impoverishment in the lives of people like her daughter who cannot occupy themselves because their span of concentration is so limited and who need constant involvement in activities as well as companionship of people who enjoy the same things.' (Mencap representative).

On the other hand, there is the view that both parents and the 'community' (meaning neighbours) adapt and become more accepting of group homes given good preliminary public relations work by the professionals.

'Originally attitudes were difficult but the group home had a Christmas party to which half the street and the children in the street were invited and attended. As a result public awareness and cooperation increased.' (hospital administrator).

'Younger parents and most older parents can accept community living if they are persuaded adequately, with counselling, although most want hostels; some middle-class parents are the exception as they firmly want the kind of special village community that exists; in contrast the mentally handicapped are 100% pleased with community preferences.' (social services adviser).

Neighbours can be awkward and uneasy without the help of service providers to show the relative ease with which to deal with clients as non-handicapped people interact with their neighbours. Yet some argue that community attitudes vary only from apathy to hostility and rarely to genuine understanding. Parents talk of friends disappearing as soon as their child's problem becomes apparent; hence this influences their view on whether the 'community' is prepared to accept the handicapped in a more general sense.

The point regarding the need to offer counselling to parents is well-rehearsed; equally in the context of neighbourhood acceptance the argument appears to be that 'most' neighbours will accept the handicapped provided that explanation is given to them of the nature of the undertaking — 'familiarity outbreeds contempt'. One parent remarks that 'community attitudes are easier in urban areas, probably due to there being less involvement between neighbours and more difficult in villages and small towns where mentally handicapped people stand out and there are not enough things for them to do e.g. shop-gazing, tea/coffee drinking.' Experience of setting up group homes in Chesterfield, Derbyshire has showed how some local people became 'fed-up' as they resented the fact that the mentally handicapped residents expected an awful lot of help from them 'in the same way as they had been accustomed to receive help from the hostel........ They would knock on doors asking for tablets if they had a headache instead of doing things for themselves. As a result the neighbours became harrassed with the attitude "oh no, not another home"'.

In conclusion, the overwhelming view tends in favour of parental opposition or apprehension regarding group homes, in spite of professional counselling. This is heightened by parents' beliefs that many professionals fail to appreciate their feelings which gives rise to an added source of tension between the two sides. It is a statutory obligation on the part of local authorities to consider the views of parents in community placements of this kind.

Throughout the above, there has been reference to a number of vital issues in the development of group homes for mentally handicapped adults. The policy initiative is clear: both the White Paper review and the Green Paper 'Care in the Community' declare that more handicapped adults should be cared for in ordinary housing accommodation and that priority needs to be given to making resources available for this transfer. The will is there and the initiative is left in the hands of the local authorities. Reference has been made to the following considerations: the selection of residents suitable for group home care, the preparation for living and staff support needed, the problem of adjusting to community living and the views of parents in the context of those of the wider community. Finally there is the matter of daily occupation: most residents in group homes attend either ATC or else are in open employment. If quality of life is to be enhanced for residents then proper contacts are required between residential and day care authorities involving the use of planned educational and training programmes. Experience has proved that many residents are able to control their own finances following consistent and well-structured teaching, whilst favourable benefit rates can be organised with the DHSS when the group home is linked to a statutory support agency. Successful day-to-day living depends much on the aggregate of personalities of members forming the group: the 'group harmony' factor is worthy of serious consideration within selection policies. Residents, furthermore, require social and recreational pastimes or, at least, there is a requirement for a means of combatting felt anxieties of parents concerning the inability of mentally handicapped people to concentrate on prepared activities. The question might be 'should care staff be responsible for providing activities for residents to fill their non-working hours, including, for example, a programme to ensure that residents maintain the upkeep of the house?' The alternative might be that residents are left to 'loaf around' the home, with opportunities for allowing the state of the house to deteriorate, for them to overspend on their weekly allowance or simply to 'hang around' the neighbourhood aimlessly, maybe making a nuisance of themselves. This is particularly important as mentally handicapped people may *not* be tolerated in social situations where the non-handicapped may be allowed to escape from blame; there being a firm onus on the former to abide by acceptable social norms. This must underline the evident stigma for clients of being associated with mental handicap services: no wonder that some parents feel justified in rejecting this association.

CHAPTER 2

Introduction to the Study

Progress in the development of non-institutionalised residential care for mentally handicapped adults has been both slow and lacking in direction. Group home provision on a national basis has been limited partly by the absence of commitment on the part of health and social service departments and partly by a lack of research evidence on the relevant issues, for example, the suitable range and mix of residents, the nature of community support, the type of staffing and its organisation. The Sheffield Development Project (SDP) created an opportunity for the study of some of these issues. The SDP recommended the introduction of a range of new residential units to meet the needs of three categories of client, described as:

'A. Those who, because of additional heavy physical handicaps or severe behaviour problems, require the support of a full hospital service fairly close at hand;

B. Those who, because of less obvious physical handicaps, possibly some degree of incontinence and behaviour problems, require limited medical and nursing supervision, and

C. Those who could be cared for within a normal home if such a home was available to them.'

These were to be provided for respectively in AHA hospital units; AHA hostels; and LA hostels and group homes. The main focus of this study is on residents living in LA group homes but some comparisons are drawn with those living in LA hostels as these are intended to cater for the same type of mentally handicapped adult.

A main purpose of the study was to select, on the basis of other research and documented evidence, factors which are important determinants of the successful operation and outcome of group homes. Residential care in Sheffield has until relatively recently been provided in hospital and hostel accommodation for groups ranging from 20 to over 200 residents with full-time staffing support. The authorities in Sheffield during 1974–77 provided 29 places in 6 group homes, these being ordinary houses situated in different areas within the city boundary. Residents had entered the group homes from either a hospital or hostel; all but two homes were single-sexed, the exceptions having four females and one male, three females and two males; of the other four homes three comprised female residents and the other male. The age range varied throughout although

25

approximately one half of the residents fell within the 31–50 age range and 10 were 60 plus. Residents living in these houses received part-time support by visits from Social Workers and Home Helps. This constituted an experiment on the part of the Local Authority, hence the study aimed also to look at the evolution of the homes from a professional and administrative standpoint, and to discover how the main providing authority, the Social Services Department, adapted and adjusted its resources to deal with the scheme. A number of questions emerged, for example, what criteria should be used to determine the 'success' of a group home? What were the aims of the administrative and support agencies? What methods did they employ?

Despite the formal policy recommendation of the Sheffield Feasibility Study Report (FSR) that the LA should provide places in both hostels and groups homes for 'those (mentally handicapped adults) who could be cared for within a normal home if such a home was available to them', the assumption was that residents in group homes would be found to be more able than those in hostels. The intention was to test this formally by comparing the abilities of residents within both types of unit, but the timing of the research precluded an assessment of group home residents at the point at which they were being moved into the homes. All the same it was decided to carry out an assessment on the two groups to observe any major differences between them. It was also decided to reassess group home residents two years after the initial assessment in order to determine whether any change had occurred, and then to analyse reasons for this change. For example, the official outside support received by residents was investigated to determine whether and how this had changed over the two year period, if so what had been the reasons for its change and whether specifically these changes could justifiably be related to changes in the assessment scores of residents on both an individual and group basis.

Two testable hypotheses were formulated — firstly, that residents placed in group homes would be more able than residents in hostels, and secondly, that residents in group homes receiving high staff support would make more positive gains on the assessment instrument than those with low staff support. The nature of staffing support given to the homes before the period in question and during it was recorded and analysed, data being gathered in a variety of ways in an attempt to obtain the most comprehensive picture possible under the circumstances. Informal contacts were maintained with all members of staff providing direct support to homes, staff meetings were attended, staff at all levels were interviewed, departmental files and diaries were studied and analysed and regular frequent visits were made by the author to the homes where both staff and residents were seen.

In addition to looking at the assessment scores of the group home residents, it was also decided to look at group interaction and informal support networks, both of which might affect the success of a group home. This analysis was relevant also in terms of the specific aim of trying to account for changes in individual residents by the two-year reassessment. The files contained information on their previous background and these were examined in order to see if there were any indications of possible links between 'successful' group home placement and previous background experience.

A study of group interaction was considered to be important due to the fact that the provision of limited external support to residents on a visiting basis was unusual in the context of traditional residential care provision and it placed a heavy emphasis on the need for mutual self-help and interdependence among the residents themselves. The extent to which residents were able to mix successfully, tolerate one another and organise themselves in accomplishing certain household tasks had serious implications for the amount of support they would require and for the success of the group home in general. It was important to assess what internal factors enabled the groups to cohere, whether group home living presented particular problems for individuals and what role was played by both residents and support staff in solving any problems that arose.

The ideal method for dealing with this was to 'live among' the residents of each group home for a fixed time period and to observe their behaviour through participation in various activities. This was discarded, however, due to the amount of time considered necessary to carry it out and instead a method of paying regular visits to each home was used, involving much time spent with residents, either chatting informally with a group or with individuals, performing household jobs together or simply joining them to watch TV. The intention was to develop a picture in terms of the strengths and weaknesses of individual personalities in the context of the group's need to maintain a certain level of harmony in order to survive.

Another important factor to consider in looking at the success of a group home is the amount and type of informal support that it receives. It was anticipated that residents would have made some contacts with local people but that the nature and range of these would depend on individual circumstances, for example, the action of official support agencies or the type of neighbourhood. There was also the probability that other social contacts existed, for example, friends and relatives and that, taken together, this informal source of contact and support would affect the amount of official support needed. It was virtually impossible to determine accurately a group's need for official support from the standpoint of determining what informal support was available. For example, while it was possible to question individual residents on what outside informal contacts they received and to go further and observe some of these interactions, it was no easy task to evaluate the overall significance of these contacts in the context of the need for support from an alternative source.

Without the encouragement of the official support services to muster informal support to the homes, it is likely that this latter would be limited, meaning that it would be substantially less than that provided through official channels and that without this sort of official intervention it would also be dependent on random factors. A first step towards determining the nature and range of informal support, as opposed to official support, was to ask the residents themselves questions about contacts they made and help they received. It would then be possible to enlarge on this pool of information by following up and questioning the individuals referred to. The present study only went as far as taking the initial step of interviewing residents, although this was done both formally and informally. It was decided not to collect comparable data from residents living in hostels, for example, but instead to restrict the investigation to a critical analysis of data provided through discussions with the group home residents and to cast this in the light of data obtained from other source material.

In summary, this research has two general aims, to study:

a. the residents of the group homes (see 1–6 below) and

b. the official support they receive (see 7–9 below).

The specific aims of the study are as follows:

1. to establish whether the type of previous placement had influenced the success of a resident's placement in a group home

2. to identify differences in the pattern and range of abilities of residents in LA hostels and group homes

3. to ascertain whether the abilities and behaviours of the group home residents improve, deteriorate or remain constant

4. to examine the effects of group interactions

5. to identify problems, if any, which developed between residents within the group homes

6. to examine the knowledge and attitudes of residents to community contacts and support

7. to investigate administrative and decision-making processes by professionals outside the group homes

8. to identify criteria used to place the residents in a group home

9. to investigate the type and amount of support given to the group home residents by professional staff and others.

Comparative data have been collected on the six Sheffield group homes, using the following methods:

1. a documentary file search on the background history of residents, the professional assessments made of them and administrative decision-making

2. participant observation in the homes involving in addition formal interviews with all the residents

3. maintaining regular contact with a range of support staff, conducting formal

interviews with members of each support 'team' and attendance at staff meetings

4. the assessment, using an established instrument, of the abilities of both residents living within the homes and in hostels; a follow-up assessment on the group home residents.

In the light of the foregoing it may be useful in the interests of clarity to couch the aims in terms of formal hypotheses:

1. that the residents of the group homes will be more able, as measured on the Adaptive Behaviour Scale (ABS), than those in hostels

2. that residents in group homes having a high support staff-resident ratio will show greater gains on the ABS than those with less favourable support-staff-resident ratios

3. that group behaviour factors affect the success/failure of a group home

4. that the majority of outside support given to residents is through official support channels rather than through informal and neighbourhood contacts.

It was decided to organise the material under two main headings: the first dealing with the issues relating to facts on the residents and their internal perspectives — their background experience, their abilities, the relationships and interactions of individual residents within the homes, their expressed contacts and support; the second with the official support network, taken from an alternative professional and administrative viewpoint using documentary and interview sources.

CHAPTER 3

The Residents

This section presents a range of data on the residents of the group homes (to be referred to as GH1 to 6). Firstly, it summarises data taken from their individual casefiles relating to their previous experience with specific regard to residential placement. Secondly, it presents the assessment scores of residents, initially comparing them with a sample from LA hostels and then showing the results of a two-year follow-up. The third part deals with resident interaction within each of the group homes, showing the results of a study using participant-observation. The final part presents the findings of interviews with residents concerning their outside contacts.

SECTION 1

Their Previous Background History

Since the start a total of 33 residents had lived in the six group homes and individual case files were available for all but one of them. However, it was clear that the material in each file differed markedly in quality and in no case was it evident that all the information on file about the history of a resident had 'travelled with' him. As a generalisation the record-keeping was patchy and in several cases gave no insight whatsoever of the early background history and reasons for residential care of the individuals concerned. In the case of files maintained at the Social Services Department, all were studied and additionally hospital files for particular individuals where these were available on request.

Individuals who had previously resided in hospital had frequently moved from one hospital unit to another during their total length of stay. These residents who had been in one of the old hospital units had usually spent time in its domestic training unit (DTU) and this applied particularly to GH3 residents. Five residents had on at least one occasion been moved from hospital to hostel 'on trial' but had to be returned to hospital. Several residents had previously lived in non-mental handicap units, for example, two residents had served long sentences in penal units having been convicted of criminal offences, whereas two others had been taken into Local Authority care under

Section I of the 1948 Children Act and in this regard had been moved from one unit to another before being placed in a mental handicap unit. A further resident had first been placed in a hostel for the mentally ill, then into an ordinary flat in the community and then returned to the same hostel. The most prevailing reason for residential care in the first place was the ill health/disability or death of a caring relative, usually a parent but in other cases, an aunt, grandmother, brother ot stepfather. This applied in at least 16 of the 33 cases studied.

'Following (this) death it was clear that Ian was unable to look after himself and the family could not offer adequate care and support. Enquiries made within the Social Services Department for a bed in a hostel were unsuccessful or there were no vacancies......contacted the Medical Consultant and arrangements were made for movement to (hospital)......' (Social Work Report).

In 5 cases there had been no information at all relating to why the person had been admitted into residential care and in certain other cases the reasons for their being admitted from a different type of unit to a mental handicap unit were very difficult to fathom. One girl having been placed under a Local Authority Order at the age of fifteen was, three years later, following medical recommendation, moved to a hospital for the mentally handicapped:

'......The problem concerns her spoilt behaviour which lacks discipline and control. She would play her parents off against each other. Another trait which is of interest is that she seems to prefer male garments......talks of being raped, dramatises and romanticises situations. She is therefore a very mixed-up child and a very unreliable one. She appears to have a male orientation and finds female figures a difficult and social problem. Her behaviour is likely to be dominated by self-gratification, rather than in the fashion of a young adult. She would in any institutional situation be a disturbing influence. I consider that she would be unsuitable for the girls' hostel and would think that if it were possible for her to continue her employment she might be suitable for a hospital for the subnormal where there is more discipline and supervision.'

There were 3 cases where giving birth to an illegitimate child had contributed strongly to the person being taken into residential care. These were women who had been 'ascertained' under the first Mental Deficiency Act (1913) and in one noted case had also at the time been 'in receipt of poor relief'.

'......Gladys was delivered of her first illegitimate child on 16 December 1935. The child died on 31 December 1935. The mother asked for Gladys to be given another chance at home and promised to give her good care. This was agreed to but despite frequent visits by the Local Authority and repeated warnings to both parents and Gladys, she again became pregnant, this time by a married man. The Local Authority are now of the opinion that "it is in the best interests of the defective that she should be placed in an institution".'

Another was placed in care having been 'subject to be dealt with under the same Act......by reason of the following circumstances: she is found neglected'. She had been wandering the streets at night and on occasions staying out which had created problems for the person(s) caring for her resulting eventually in an offer of hospitalisation being accepted. In at least one other case, the caring relative had taken up this kind of offer owing to an inability to cope with the mentally handicapped person's disturbed or difficult behaviour in the home situation.

Few details were available on the earlier background of residents, for example, there were 12 cases where it was stated that they had attended 'special school' and 3 where they had remained at ordinary school during childhood. In the first they had been 'ascertained' under the Act and 'labelled' under the legal nomenclature. There were two cases where it was found that residents had been 'excluded' from school.

'He is unfit for school, making no progress. He can't attend to himself at the lavatory; has a low IQ; is ineducable at any school.'

In three cases there was reference to there being a mentally handicapped sibling in the family and there were other occasional references to poor home background comprising such things as substandard housing, unemployment of father or marital disharmony. The low intellectual capacity of both parents was also mentioned.

'......both her mother and stepfather are of poor intellect and not able to give proper care. The mother resents any interference by the Local Authority and seems to encourage her to go with men.'

There was resistance on the part of the caring relative towards accepting residential care or help of any kind, owing to an overprotective attitude or a desire to maintain the person at home because of the practical help she provided.

'Sylvia is well, there is no apparent change; she runs errands and does jobs around the house. Nothing has been done regarding getting her a job, though I am quite of the opinion that this girl could be usefully employed. Her mother is a bit reluctant about a job as she's nervous about letting Sylvia go far alone.'

The files stated that 7 residents had jobs in open employment prior to their move to a group home, 4 of whom moved to the same home. Professional judgements made of residents whilst in residential care prior to the group home were often more negative than positive:

'She is unstable, emotional, quite a troublemaker.'

'She is severely subnormal in that her intelligence is under-average and she is unable to lead an independent life. She is very slow and unlikely to hold down a job.'

'She is illiterate and grossly ignorant and is unable to count the fingers of one hand. She is childish, completely institutionalised and incapable of leading an independent life.'

32

Judging from these comments it is surprising that such residents were ever chosen to live in a group home.

In summary: they had very varied backgrounds and experiences, none came directly from home, slightly over half came from hospital, slightly under half from a hostel and the remaining two (from an overall total of thirty-three present and ex-residents) from non-mental handicap residential units. Six had entered a group home along a traditional route, having gone from home to hospital to hostel first of all; almost half (16 out of 33) had spent ten or more years previously in hospital (including 9 of the 11 residents from GH2 and 3) and seven had, at least at one time in their life, been in a non-mental handicap residential unit such as a mental illness hospital or a penal unit. There was evidence to show that five had 'failed' in the past in a hostel having had to be returned to hospital; two had spent more than ten years in a penal unit for criminal offences and two others had, as children, been placed in the statutory care of the Local Authority (under Section I of the 1948 Children Act). Almost half (16 out of 33) at least, had come into residential care in the first place through the failing health or death of a caring relative; the inability of relatives to cope with the difficult and/or disturbed behaviour of the mentally handicapped person or her early 'ascertainment' under the old 1913 legislation influencing the Authorities not to take risks had been salient factors.

Whilst it had been relatively clear under what circumstances clients had come into residential care, it had not always been as clear as to why they had been admitted to a mental handicap unit. In at least three cases, residents had attended normal school during childhood; the others had received special education though this did not appear to account for the whole group, several of whom had been excluded from education. The files had remarked on the poor home circumstances of some clients as they had on the absolute refusal of certain relatives to accept residential care, or even any other services for the mentally handicapped person whilst they, the relatives, still had the ability to cope. Seven of the total group of thirty-three had jobs in open employment prior to their move to a group home. Finally, the files had contained many professional judgements made on residents whilst in previous residential care that had been negative in describing their potential for managing to live within the community.

SECTION 2

An Assessment of their Abilities

It had been envisaged that the Sheffield Development Project should provide a range of adult residential units that would meet the needs of different types of client. The sample survey reported in ERG Reports,

No. 4.* was concerned with applying the Adaptive-Behaviour Scale measurement to identify the actual range of abilities present in each residential environment and examine whether a clearly delineated range existed in practice between the various types of accommodation. Owing, however, to the small size of the group home sample preventing any useful conclusions being drawn, it was decided to assess all group home residents and to compare them with the LA hostel sample. The results of this comparison are summarised below, with the full results given in Appendix A. The results of a two-year follow-up on group home residents are presented and summarised.

(i) *The sample survey*

As stated in the above-mentioned report, the sample of group home residents tended to vary in ability between being similar to that of the hostels or being at a slightly higher level. It is important to know in what particular ways the sample of Local Authority group home residents differed from that of Local Authority hostel residents as an initial approach towards establishing the existence of Departmental policy relating to client selection. It is clear from the report that unlike the Local Authority hostels, the group homes did no have resident staff. As a result, therefore, of residents' greater opportunities for independent living, it is probable that more accurate staff ratings of their individual potential could be made than would be the case in a more protective residential setting. This is a problem in terms of drawing any final conclusion on the relative abilities of the two samples, and is particularly relevant to Part I of the Adaptive Behaviour Scale.

Referring to the above results certain domains in both Parts I and II, however, stand out as being areas where relatively clear differences emerge between the samples. For Part I these are Independent Functioning, Economic Activity, Numbers and Time and Domestic Activity. In each of these the group home sample taken as a whole, produced scores markedly higher than the Local Authority hostel one. These domains cover a number of separate skill items, for example, Independent Functioning includes a variety of self-care tasks such as eating, cleanliness and toilet use. A sub-domain such as Eating includes use of table utensils, eating in public, drinking and table manners with what appears to be a strong bias towards socially acceptable eating habits. The lack of any statistical analysis of the overall results given in the tables of the above-mentioned report precludes proper investigation into the meaning of the scores and hence the relative importance of particular sub-domains for the sample as a whole.

In Part II the domains Withdrawal, Inappropriate Interpersonal

---

* Residential Care for Mentally Handicapped Adults — Stage 1, ERG Reports, No. 4, Evaluation Research Group, Department of Psychology, University of Sheffield, 1979.

Manners and Sexually Aberrant Behaviour stand out as being areas where group home scores were markedly better. The first, Withdrawal, includes timidness, unresponsiveness, unawareness and apathy and has obviously important implications fo social interactions in a small group situation. Whereas extreme forms of this kind of behaviour can be tolerated and hidden in a larger group setting, they are clearly more noticeable and far less tolerable in a very small group. The second area, Inappropriate Interpersonal Manners, covers the following: talks too close to others' faces, blows on others faces, burps at others, kisses or licks others, hugs or squeezes others, touches others inappropriately, hangs on to others and does not let go. Some of these, for example, hangs on to others and does not let go, are typical behaviours often associated with the mentally handicapped. In general, however, they are not normally permitted in a social situation. If living in the community means making use of the normal community services then the exhibition of such behaviours as these would not be tolerated. The last area is Sexually Aberrant Behaviour and includes: engages in inappropriate masturbation, exposes body improperly, has homosexual tendencies, unacceptable sexual behaviour and suchlike. Again these are behaviours strictly unacceptable in society at large and so would not be tolerated in an unsupervised setting. The contrast between the two samples has been particularly clear as five out of six group home people scored 0 in this domain as opposed to only twelve out of twenty-five in the hostels. (No score is a rating that signifies no evidence whatsoever of Sexually Aberrant Behaviour).

(ii) *A comparison of all group home residents with a sample from LA hostels*

It was decided to take the rated ability levels of the whole population of group home residents to see how they compared with the above Local Authority hostel sample and specifically to discover whether the same domains emerged as the primary basis of contrast between these two groups. (Table 1, see next page.)

The obvious difference between the two types of unit is in the sex imbalance of residents (48 per cent of the LA sample as compared to only 20 per cent of the GH one are males). The sample taken from LAs accurately reflects their total population. It may be that females are considered more suitable for group home living owing to normal expectations concerning their role as housekeeper. (Table 2, see next page.)

The first point is that the sample from the Local Authority hostels is not representative of the total hostel population. The other is that the two samples are not strictly comparable on an age basis: the group home residents are in the main noticeably older than the hostel ones, with more than 40 per cent of the former aged over 60. Reasons for this

Table 1 Sex of residents in sample and total
   (LA hostels and group homes)

Unit	Sample		Total	
	Males	*Females*	*Males*	*Females*
LA1	4	—	15	—
LA2	—	4	—	12
LA3	4	4	15	15
LA4	2	2	8	12
LA5	2	3	10	11
TOTAL LA Hostels	12	13	48	50
gh1	—	5	—	5
gh2	1	4	1	4
gh3	2	3	2	3
gh4	—	3	—	3
gh5	—	5	—	5
gh6	1	—	1	—
TOTAL Group Homes	4	20	4	20

Table 2 Age of residents in sample and total
   (LA hostels and group homes)

		16–30	*31–45*	*46–50*	*60+*
LA Hostels	— Total	40	26	27	5
	— Sample	7	6	11	1
Group Homes	— Total	1	6	7	10
	— Sample	1	6	7	10

are not clear though it may have been thought that people of retirement age would present fewer behaviour or management problems to staff and hence be reasonably settled in an unrestrictive environment.

The full results of the assessment are set out in Appendix A and can be summarised as follows:

Scores for group home residents on Part I of the Scale, taken overall, are higher than those for hostel residents, with particular emphasis on domains headed Economic Activity, Language Development, Numbers and Time and Domestic Activity. However, the scores of group home residents on individual sections of each sub-domain tended to follow one of two patterns: they either show considerable variation within the total resident group, for example, money handling, writing or else they are high throughout, for example, pre-verbal expression, conversation, table clearing. In Part II, scores for group home and hostel residents are very similar with overall low scores (i.e. few 'maladaptive behaviours') being made. There are five sub-domains, however, where half or more of the group home population scored. Both in these and in other domains/sub-domains residents from GH2, 3 and 5 featured far more frequently than those from the other homes and two residents stood out as scoring twice as often as the majority of the remainder.

(iii) *A follow-up assessment*

The follow-up took place exactly two years after the initial assessment. There had been few changes in the group home population during this period. These had consisted of the following: two from GH5 had died (Mary Hemsley, Beattie James) and one had moved alone into a flat (Lily Nichols); another resident had moved into GH5 and a further one into GH4. The follow-up assessment was carried out on those originally assessed, a total of twenty-one residents. The following chart shows changes for each resident by each domain. It indicates 'improvement', 'deterioration', or 'no change' for each resident/domain. (Note 'improvement' in Part I domain scores is signified by a higher score and in Part II by a lower one; 'deterioration' is vice-versa).

The chart shows a mixture of trends with some clear indications: the overall pattern for GH1 is of 'no change' with clearest improvements on Responsibility and Psychological Disturbances; the overall pattern for GH2 is of 'improvement' with all residents having improved on Independent Functioning, Economic Activity, Socialisation, Antisocial Behaviour, Untrustworthy Behaviour, Unacceptable and Eccentric Habits and Psychological Disturbances; the overall pattern for GH4 is of 'deterioration' with all residents having deteriorated on Economic Activity, Self-direction, and Psychological Disturbances. Looking at the total resident group, *one half or more* improved in Independent Functioning, Economic Activity, Responsibility, Socialisation, Rebellious Behaviour and Psychological Disturbances; *one quarter or more* deteriorated on Independent Functioning, Physical Development, Economic Activity, Language Development, Numbers and Time, Vocational Activity, Self-direction, Rebellious Behaviour, Untrustworthy Behaviour and Psychological Disturbances.

A breakdown of individual 'improvements/deteriorations' by each sub-domain shows that *one half or more* of the total resident group improved on: Posture, Clothing, Public Transportation, Money Handling, Table Setting, Persistence, General Responsibility, Consideration for Others, Lies or Cheats, and Reacts Poorly to Criticism. Looking at the two homes (GH2 and 4) where clearer indications of overall change occurred: at GH2 *all* residents improved on Miscellaneous Independent Functioning, Persistence, Interaction with Others, Teases or Gossips

Legend:
- ☐ Improvement
- ■ Deterioration
- ▨ No Change

Groups and names (columns):

GH1	Barbara Anson, Sylvia Beck, Brenda Marston, Doris Shelley, Barbara Turnsip, Doris Grantham, Beryl Hirt
GH2	Doris Lampton, John Rylands, Violet Rylands
GH3	Gladys Smallfield, Beattie Thomas, Ronnie Talbot, Bertha Houghton, George Maybury
GH4	Doreen Brampton, Ruth Green, Shirley Weston
GH5	Maud Aughton, Audrey Tinsley
GH6	Henry Hunter

Categories (rows):
- Indep. Func.
- Physical Develpmnt.
- Econ. Activity
- Lang. Develpmnt.
- Numbers & Time
- Domestic Activity
- Voc. Activity*
- Self-direction
- Responsibility
- Socialisation
- Violent & Des. Beh.
- Antisocial Behav.
- Rebellious Behav.
- Untrustworthy Behav.
- Withdrawal
- Stereo Beh. & Odd Manner
- Inapp. Interp. Manners
- Unaccept. Voc. Habits
- Unaccept./Eccentric Hab.
- Self-abusive Behav.
- Hyperactive Tend.
- Sex. Abber. Behav.
- Psychological Disturb.
- Use of Medication

38

about Others and Lies and Cheats. *Four of the five* residents at GH2 improved on Clothing, Money Handling, Budgeting, Purchasing, Job Performance, Consideration for Others, Participation in Group Activities, Has Disturbing Vocal or Speech Habits, Reacts Poorly to Frustration and Demands Excessive Attention or Praise. At GH4 *all* deteriorated on Telephone, Money Handling, Errands, Word Usage, Time, Passivity and Reacts Poorly to Criticism.

Many residents improved or learned new skills relating to community adjustment and group living. At GH2 there was an overall improvement in group living skills — consideration for others, group participation and individual 'maladaptive behaviour'. Improvements throughout were in areas commonly associated with independent community living — clothing, money handling, budgeting, purchasing (from shops and local facilities). GH4 showed deterioration in a number of areas not identifiable in terms of overall trend.

(iv) *Summary*

Following an assessment of all the group home residents on the A-B Scale, it was shown that in Part I domains group home resident scores had been decisively higher (better) than those of LA hostel residents — particularly striking differences in domains Economic Activity, Language Development, Numbers and Time and Domestic Activity, and that in Part II domains the scores of the two groups had been similar — with overall low scores, indicating few 'maladaptive' behaviours in both groups. Individual group home residents had been followed-up two years later to determine what, if any, changes had taken place in their assessment scores. Apart from random changes in the different domain scores of residents, patterns had emerged in relation to three homes: an overall 'no change' at GH1, 'improvement' at GH2 and 'deterioration' at GH4. Taking the total resident population as a whole, one half or more had improved on six out of the twenty-four domains. Looking at changes in individuals at sub-domain level, one half or more had improved in such skill areas as use of public transport, money handling, general responsibility and consideration for others. Overall improvements had occurred at GH2 in two main areas — group interaction (consideration for others, participation, individual behaviour) and the use of money (money handling, purchasing, budgeting). Overall deterioration at GH4 occurred in areas of learned behaviour such as use of telephone, telling the time and money handling.

SECTION 3

Factors in Group Living

(i) *Introduction*

'It might be trite to say that the members of a group bring to it their previous experience and share with one another the experience of being part of a group. The members *are* the group: the influence of the group upon them may be great or small, but one thing is certain, there are influences at work, whatever the experience and knowledge of the individual may be'. (Douglas, p. 130).

The purpose of this section is to overview the interpersonal relationships of group home residents using the framework of group dynamics. Data were collected over a two and one half year period, using a participant-observation approach. Each home was visited approximately every three weeks during the first year, and then every two months, resulting in at least twenty-five visits being made to each group home. The research worker did not visit by arrangement nor at necessarily routine times, although for GH1 and 4 where all residents were out during the day, visits were made in the early evening, with weekend visits also included. Most visits were made alone, although one some occasions the research worker was accompanied by one of the social work staff.

The research worker had originally been introduced to the residents of each home by one of the visiting support team, and described to them as someone doing research on group homes ('someone interested in how people live together as a group') who worked at the University and who wanted to make regular visits to their homes ('he wants to "drop in" and see you from time to time if it's all right'). The object, from the point of view of the research worker, was to build up a trusting and friendly relationship with residents over the course of time. The majority of visits were for the duration of one to two hours, sometimes limited by obvious circumstances like if the residents were generally busy, about to serve meals, or were on the point of going out somewhere. The procedure (if it could be referred to as such) was for the research worker to 'chat' about everyday events and try and give the residents an opportunity to talk about what they liked. During the course of the visits there were also opportunities for discussion with individuals, sometimes on a confidential basis.

An original aim had been to offer one's services in the form of practical help, but opportunities for this turned out to be rare on the whole and consisted, for example, of giving someone a 'lift', collecting an item from a local shop or making a pot of tea. It seemed that residents enjoyed having a 'guest' to whom they could show off their latest acquisitions, with whom they could 'talk over' a problem or simply 'chat' in a friendly way. Immediately following each visit, notes were scribbled into a 'diary' and added to on the next visit. The following analysis is based on the 'diary' kept for each home.

At the time of the research study, residents of each home were engaged during weekdays in the following way:

40

	Open Employment	ATC	At home
GH1	3	2	
GH2		2	3
GH3	1		4
GH4		3	
GH5	2	3	
GH6		1	

(ii) Sharing

In order to survive the group must live as a cohesive unit; there are factors which promote cohesion such as the sharing of common experiences, attitudes and expectations. For a group to live together certain aspects of their life must be organised and in particular this concerns the basic division of household tasks and use of facilities within the homes. For example, there must be an understanding of how the facilities of the home are used and shared, and given that tasks are needed for the maintenance and survival of the group home, an understanding must evolve among members for the purposes of seeing that these are carried out.

(a) *Sharing housing tasks:* in all cases it was recognised that certain tasks need to be carried out to keep the homes on a steady footing. If a small number of people were to live together successfully then basic housework tasks needed to be organised. Two main procedures emerged in relation to the present homes: the taking of roles and the rota system.

Role-taking — In four homes (GH1, 2, 3 and 5) it was clear that certain group members had their own 'jobs' whether it was for example, cooking the evening or mid-day meal, cleaning the house, shopping or doing the washing. These arrangements had usually been derived from initial agreement and reflected the status and identity granted to certain individual residents. In GH2 and 3 this type of role-taking involved only the female members of the group and centred around specific household tasks such as those mentioned above. The implication was that the women jointly played the housekeeping role and it was assumed in both of these cases that a male member of this group should in turn be responsible for the upkeep of the garden. In GH2 this was a plausible assumption — John Rylands maintained the garden to a high standard, boasting a rich variety of vegetables with other patches well cultivated. This was an interest nurtured during his long residence in hospital and did not constitute a 'chore' on his part. He was assisted by Doris Lampton who was also keenly interested in gardening. In GH3 unfortunately the situation was rather different — one of the two males was nominally

41

responsible for the upkeep of the garden but had neglected it to such an extent that it had become overgrown and beyond short-term treatment.

In GH1 the practice of allocating specific jobs to different people had grown out of the original rota system whereby each resident did a different job each week. The present system was more convenient to the group in that it 'fitted in' with any private arrangements they were likely to make. It did not, however, cover all household tasks and left some, for example, shopping to be still undertaken on a rotational basis. Doris Shelley prepared the 'tea' every night for the other residents. She worked as a cleaner in a small nearby hospital with hours normally from 7 a.m. to 3.30 p.m., allowing her ample time to return home and prepare a meal for the others, three of whom worked later hours. Sylvia Beck would assist in the washing-up though occasionally she would be absent, having made alternative arrangements elsewhere. Doris was rather a fussy individual and liked the others to appear at a set time for their meal, usually around half-past five, whereupon she would present the fruits of her labours to a hopefully already seated group. Furthermore, she considered herself a reasonable cook (probably superior to the rest, apart perhaps from Barbara Anson) and hence properly justified in taking over this responsibility. Barbara Anson and Brenda Marston had weekend house jobs, cleaning the rooms and doing the washing respectively. The benefit to the individual of this arrangement was that it left her free and uncommitted for the rest of the week. This is not to suggest, however, that the situation in this home was static as changes had occurred within it, for example, as the group had no washing machine, Brenda had to use the launderette down the road. One day she returned the washing insufficiently dried much to the dismay of one resident who thereupon insisted on doing it herself as from then on. This arrangement however only lasted a relatively short time but illustrates nonetheless the implausibility in practical terms of giving individuals final responsibility for specific jobs in the home.

At GH2, 3 and 5 there was some acceptance of the principle that certain residents had their 'own jobs'. Only in GH3 however was this most clearly evident with respect to the women of the group. At GH2 there was constant bickering between Doris Lampton and Violet Rylands as to who should be responsible for what. Temporarily it would be agreed that the former should do all the cooking of meals but this would be disrupted following Violet's insistence on taking over the 'housekeeper' role. Equally Doris would begin to criticise Violet's ability to cook a meal properly. She would say that she was too 'messy' and that her standards were not high enough. Unlike Violet, Doris was accustomed to rising particularly early in the morning and there were often arguments over who should make the breakfast. This applied in the case of doing the washing for each would claim the right to 'take over'. In general, however, an agreeable arrangement prevailed for at

42

least a short period of time. At GH5 the business of preserving jobs for residents existed but, as with GH2, only seemed to involve two residents in particular. Cooking again was the main source of contention and whilst it was generally accepted that this was Lily Nichols' duty, from time to time Audrey Tinsley insisted on 'stepping in' and trying her hand in the kitchen. Audrey had been singled out by the Home Helps and taught to use the washing machine which effectively made her responsible for the group's washing. The others would endeavour to ensure that their rooms were kept tidy and that their main personal needs were met but much of the remaining housework was left to the Home Helps.

GH3 provided an example of a relatively harmonious group-living situation which relied heavily on the formal role-taking habits of its female members. The three female inhabitants were proud of their relative independence and exhibited this by taking their household duties very seriously. Jointly they appeared to have recognised and accepted the need to prove both to themselves and to others that they were fully capable of running a household. There was no real evidence of mutual antagonism with respect to the fulfilment of these roles, neither was there serious resentment towards the males for their relative non-participation. The issue of asserting their independence took precedence and outweighed any other feelings they might have borne. Gladys Smallfield managed the finances, the shopping, the washing and shared in the cleaning. Beattie Thomas ran errands, accompanied Gladys to the shops, did most of the washing-up and shared in the cleaning and tidying-up of the house. Bertha was, first and foremost, the cook although she did contribute to cleaning arrangements for the house. In all they seem to have managed these jobs successfully without treading on one another's toes. Bertha got up at 5 a.m. every morning in order to make George's breakfast before he left for work.

'I get up an' make breakfast for George to get him off to work, then I tidy up and have a wash, an' make breakfast for the others, an' later I make a cooked dinner an' get the tea ready. I do all the cooking.'

In addition to the daily meal routines Bertha made tea or coffee for the group at set times during the day. She would be keen to boast of her capabilities in the kitchen and, in doing so, would consistently look to the others for confirmation of her claim.

Rota system — In three of the homes (GH1, 2 and 4) residents had, at one stage at least, resorted to a rota system for ensuring that certain tasks were carried out. At GH1 and 4 this formed the basis of the initial arrangements made for the homes and related mainly to cooking and shopping activities. A system was suggested for GH2 by one of the support workers subsequent to the admission to the home of Doris Grantham as a means of allaying potential disputes among the women

43

over their respective duties. In none of these cases did it, however, have a long-term appeal and eventually 'fizzled out' to be overtaken by either a role-taking system such as described above or some other ad-hoc arrangement. The only obvious example of its staying-power rested in the case of the weekly bulk-shopping arrangements for GH1; each Thursday evening residents took turns to go in twos to a nearby super-market. In GH2 the rota only dealt with cooking arrangements and was put aside once it became clear that Doris Grantham was failing to 'pull her weight'. This particular issue was forever a source of contention for the other two women, hence it did not take long for them to find the merest excuse to have the formal system exchanged for the original one of role-taking on at least a temporary basis.

At GH4 the activities of cooking, shopping and washing clothes were nominally organised on a rotational basis throughout the first year of the home's existence after which these became organised much less formally, although residents still tended to take turns over the daily cooking and meal preparation. The long-term survival of a rota system for household jobs depended on factors such as the extent to which it adequately served the individual needs of residents. Small group living demanded flexibility on the part of individual residents and some willingess to compromise, yet when a set arrangement such as a rota system lost its attraction for one resident in the group, then one or more of the others would follow. In GH1 it was clear that all residents were not 'at home' for every evening meal hence the rota could not operate unless, of course, individual residents were prepared to swap duties which in fact did occur in the early stages. Eventually this system proved unworkable and an informal arrangement evolved with Doris and Barbara Anson doing most of the cooking and meal preparation. Later on, as described, this became more clearly Doris' preserve.

(b) *Sharing and companionship:*   In all homes apart from GH6, some members of each group had known one another beforehand, hence the basis for group or sub-group relationships had been established. Usually residents had been living in the same hospital ward or hostel hence they had shared common experiences and relationships which contributed to their having like-minded views on some issues and generally finding it easy to 'get along' together. A degree of mutual tolerance is necessary for small group living and in specific homes this had been learned. However, the existence of sharing, mutual aid and friendliness which was evident among some residents went beyond a basic need for tolerance and acceptance. In some cases friendships had their roots in shared experiences which may have contributed to certain individuals being selected together for certain homes. Whereas these may have had positive binding effects in one sense, in another they may have resulted in the exclusion of one or more other group member (see sub-groups and scapegoating). For the present, it is important to consider the potential advantages gained from the existence of sharing and companionship within the group homes.

Sharing possessions — There is some evidence to show the extent to which personal possessions were shared in the homes. Food was shared but then it was purchased collectively, except, for example, in instances when an individual resident bought or received 'extras' such as a cake, chocolates or a bottole of sherry. Some items were paid for jointly, for example, a hairdrier and kitchen equipment whereas others strictly belonged to individuals. At GH4 Shirley had a record-player which she allowed others to use. At GH3 the female residents bought clothes which they occasionally lent to one another on social occasions. At GH2 the women shared sewing materials and sometimes borrowed money from one another.

Companionship — Some residents, particularly those whose relationships with one another were long-standing, were seen to joke frequently together, insult one another harmlessly and to show closeness of deep affection. At GH3 residents were happy with their state of living, enjoyed one another's company and encourged and complimented one another in a friendly fashion. Despite what has already been said of Violet and Doris Lampton at GH2 their relationship was basically a stable one. Occasionally they would maul each other as if like schoolgirls, playing on each other's weak spots but with ho harm intended.

Mutual aid — This can imply a number of things including, for example, the function of role-taking whereby individuals aid the group by being responsible for one or more aspects of its work, aid to individuals — usually the weaker or weakest members of the group — by one or more group members and co-operative effort whereby individuals pool information and other resources for the purpose of planning towards and achieving certain expressed goals. Role-taking has been discussed; the practice of providing proportionately more aid to less-able group members was most clearly observed in the case of GH2, 3 and 5. In GH2 Beryl was constantly 'mothered' by the two older female residents; in GH3 Beattie was given a lot of extra support from the others and this applied also, but in a more limited way, to Maud at GH5 owing to her physical disability. The residents of GH3 frequently discussed each other's problems openly, passing on information and advising one another as far as they were able. They would talk about how to obtain items, locate shops and deal with relatively complex situations such as being sold faulty goods. They would plan together: they would arrange future outings and social events for one another on occasions. They appeared to know each others' habits and preferences

45

well enough to be able to give useful advice and buy items on each others' behalf. Sharing ideas and giving advice were evident to some degree among residents of the other homes. Principal subjects for discussion were where to shop for particular items and, among the women, how to dress for social occasions.

Common experience — In most cases the residents were at least acquainted with one another prior to moving in. There were examples of residents moving to a home 'en bloc' from a particular hospital or hostel. Where this did not apply, residents still had experienced certain things in common simply by their having been a user of local mental handicap services at different stages during their life. In the case of GH2, 3 and 5 the common basis of past experience was particularly marked — residents had 'grown up' together, known the same range of people, and had been subject to the same routines and methods of treatment by official bodies. This fundamental sharing of experiences had resulted in their having at least some views in common.

Personal tastes and preferences were similar in many respects — they liked similar foods, wore similar clothes, liked similar television programmes and shared a similar social life. Attitudes and values were similar — they usually showed a similar deference to authority figures, had similar notions of the 'the normal life' and in some cases, had a similar strong desire to prove that they could run a home successfully. The shared experiences of the past contributed to the harmonious working relationships that had evolved in the homes. It appeared as if residents were aware of the strength of the common bonds between them, giving them an individual identity by being part of a group. For mentally handicapped people who have been in other types of residential care for any length of time, the difficulties of adjusting to a relatively independent life in the community cannot be overstressed. When demands are made on an individual to become part of a community and share in its life, it is all to easy to respond by withdrawing into the protective shell of the group home. For individuals to take on this challenge they need support from the group and the present study revealed several examples where the common interests and background of residents provided such valuable support.

(iii) *Internal divisions*

Each small group has divisions within it. It is not possible for total harmony to exist always; individual personalities need to express themselves and in order to survive the group must find ways of reconciling the different attitudes and interests of its members. Douglas (1976) writes, 'Conflict is an essential ingredient of human existence. Frequently this basic fact is overlooked because excessive conflict is seen to create hardship, promote aggressors, and to produce great hurt'.

46

Northen (1969) comments on the fact that conflict within a group can lead to increased understanding and an increase in trust, largely because differences are brought out into the open and cease to be a source of hidden irritation.

An instructive method of looking at the ways in which members operate within groups is to examine the roles which they occupy at different times within the group. For example, leadership acts tend to fall into two main areas of behaviour, *i.e.* those directed toward achieving the goals of the group — task oriented, and those directed toward smoothing relationships between members — socio-emotionally-oriented (Verba, 1967). The roles of all members playing a leader part fall within one or both of these categories. Because, in general, each member of a social system plays many roles it follows that they may not all be compatible and conflict develops.

(a) *Conflict between residents:* In group situations conflict may arise from several major areas. For instance when personal needs and purposes are different to the accepted needs and purpose of the group, a strong sense of frustration may well develop into conflict in order to achieve a higher level of personal satisfaction. Most of the problems concerned with acceptance and with power and its use all contain the seeds of possible conflict. Decision-making contains endless possibilities of conflict as does the exhibiting of particular endeavours on the part of individual group members.

There were many instances of petty quarrelling and few of more hard-edged conflict among particular residents. Argument and quarrel between individual residents is to be expected from time to time and should not be taken as an indication of serious instability within a group. It is only when circumstances were repeated and the situation arose where the same individuals were 'coming to blows' over the same issue or type of issue that the condition of a group became vulnerable. Several examples of conflict in the group homes were of a very arbitrary kind involving usually two individuals and concerning relatively petty issues such as the necessity of purchasing certain types of foodstuff, the frequency of using an electric fire, and the right of control over cooking arrangements. These soon resolved themselves with no serious consequences and were probably of considerable value in providing individuals with an opportunity to voice their views and to communicate with one another in some kind of constructive way.

At GH1 there were cases of individuals in 'storm in a teacup' arguments which sometimes required the intervention of the support worker. On some issues residents, temporarily at least, showed an inability to compromise — Barbara Anson reprimanded Doris and Brenda for over-using the electric fire. The group had received a bill which she considered extortionate. Doris, in particular, resented these

47

accusations, stating that she needed to have the fire on. Despite the intervention of the support worker asking them to compromise and recognise that different people had different needs, a coolness between Barbara and Doris prevailed for some time after the incident. Another disagreement arose out of an incident concerning Barbara Turnsnip and Brenda and most probably related to their different lifestyles and the consequent mutual misunderstandings that resulted. For example, Barbara was much older than Brenda, and attended a training unit whereas Brenda was settled in a steady job at a local dry cleaning factory. Whilst Barbara's pattern of daily activity was fairly routine, Brenda's was more erratic. She would arrive late for her tea, frequently be out in the evening socialising and sometimes be absentminded to an extent that would annoy Barbara. One evening Brenda was late home from work and proceeded to pick up and eat the wrong meal that Barbara had prepared. Barbara complained, and according to her, Brenda swore at her which resulted in her striking Brenda. The latter was very upset and convinced the others that she was going to leave the group. It was a while before this matter settled down.

In contrast to the type of short-term incident described above, other more longstanding conflict-prone situations existed in the home. These involved two or more individuals and were characterised by resentment, sometimes not overt, towards a person's behaviour which manifested itself periodically in relation to a particular set of circumstances. This type of conflict normally required the intervention of an appropriate support worker who would try to stabilise the situation, at least temporarily. In two of these cases there was certainly another side to the relationship for whereas individuals would be at 'loggerheads' one moment, they later on would be seen to show consideration and affection for each other. The underlying basis of the conflict did not disappear, however, and continued to manifest itself at intervals. Quarrels arose between Maud and Lily at GH5 resulting in their refusing to communicate with one another for short periods. The causes of contention were two-way: Maud's suspicion of Lily stealing and the latter's resenting Maud's inactivity. This dual conflict was particularly striking in view of the rather exclusive relationship enjoyed by the remaining members of the group. Similarly at GH2, quarrels frequently arose between Violet and Doris over their respective household responsibilities. The real basis of this conflict was unclear but it usually manifested itself in the form of criticising one another's ability to perform certain tasks adequately. Rather than resulting in a breakdown of communication between the two, they would usually both lose their temper, exchange insults and wait for John, Violet's husband, to step in and stabilise the situation.

A dynamic model of the interrelationships of the group home members is needed in order to appreciate the nature and effects of conflict particularly insofar as these are important in understanding the behaviour and attitudes of individuals. To take one example from GH1:

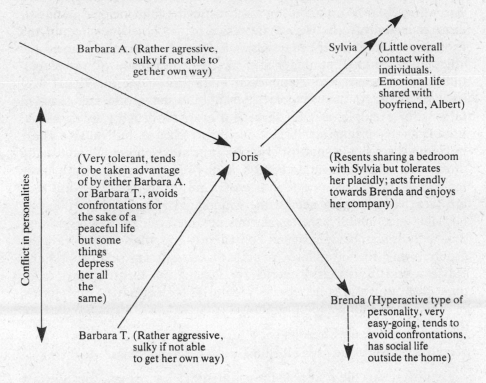

This diagram shows particular relationships existing in the home using Doris as the central figure. Whereas Doris harbours resentment towards the two Barbaras and to Sylvia for different reasons, she will only in rare cases openly confront a situation. She tends to repress her feelings, taking compensation in the fact that she has a more open friendly relationship with Brenda which she depends on a lot. It is probably true to say, however, that Doris depends on Brenda rather more than the reverse, hence the demands the former makes on the latter sometimes breed a potential conflict and distress.

(b) *Scapegoating:* Basically scapegoating is an 'off-loading' technique and the scapegoat selected to receive these attentions either has to accept because he/she has no apparent alternative, or he/she does so because this kind of attention satisfies his/her own needs. Garland and Kolodny (1970) have collected together most of the available ideas about this phenomenon which can produce distressing situations in any kind of group. Recognition of this phenomenon in a group presents little difficulty over a period of time because of its repetitive nature, the same person being made the centre of an attack at every opportunity. However, the emotional consequences of continued scapegoating are not all good, for the tendency may well develop for the group to maintain its existence at the cost of the suffering of one person.

It is possible, for example, to argue that in most small groups of the size being discussed, there is an almost inevitable tendency for one or more individuals to be viewed as 'different' by other members of the group not always for the same reasons. The present group homes provide no exception but they differ in the consistency of these relationships. Whereas, for example, at GH3 and 4 one individual may temporarily be the subject of criticism by other group members, in others, for example, at GH1 there is a more hardened view expressed uniformly by group members towards a selected individual. These individuals are singled out for criticism time and time again and usually during their absence. Garland and Kolodny remark that there are many indications that some people in a group are scapegoated because they are seen to be lagging behind the general progress of the group. At GH1, at least initially, there was considerable evidence to suggest that Sylvia Beck was being resented consistently by other members of the group owing to her failure to perform certain tasks appropriately. Sylvia would be criticised overtly for leaving the front door open at night, for not washing her clothes regularly, for not paying her rent on time, for over-eating and other things.

'She's not suitable for here, you know.' (Doris)
'You have to be behind her all the time, push her to do things.' (Barbara)

Less overt was the traditional resentment harboured towards Sylvia's general attitude and manner of presenting herself in company. For example, Sylvia would soliloquise around the house, stare fixedly at peole and objects and interrupt conversations by referring to irrelevant matters. Such behaviour was clearly annoying to the others and although it did not normally prompt their reaction, it certainly could be said to have contributed, albeit indirectly, to the formation of some sub-group activities involving specific residents. A further relevant point was the fact that Sylvia chose to spend the majority of her leisure time with her male companion, Albert. This had the effect of jeopardising the possibility of her developing close relationships with the other group members and, in fact, worked against this end insofar as the latter consistently expressed considerable antipathy towards Albert on the grounds of his having 'bad manners' and 'dirty habits'.

At GH3 George Maybury could be classed as a scapegoat for quite different reasons. Firstly, there was a clearer consensus view among other residents as to the main features of George's behaviour that they found unacceptable, and secondly, he was criticised and resented not so much for his inadequacy in performing certain tasks but rather for his conscious refusal to participate in or contribute towards the smooth running of the group home. It is possible to argue that their ability to tolerate his aberrant behaviour stemmed from the fact that they were able to work so constructively together with or without his involvement. George was criticised for his extreme meanness and idleness in the home. The others described his obsession for hoarding and hiding away money and personal possessions. He often believed that he had left them lying around the sitting-room and would proceed to search under cushions, under chairs and to grope around the floor. George later retired from his job as a general assistant at a nearby factory and began to spend more time in the home. Prior to this however, he was criticised as consistently returning home in the evening from work, demanding his meal and lying outstretched on the sofa exchanging very few words with the others. He was described as making no contribution whatsoever to general household duties, instead expecting the women to 'run around' after him. Mainly through his frequent refusal to pay Gladys his weekly rent on time (which incidentally was fixed at the same amount as that paid by other residents, even when he was working) and his appropriating unnecessary food rations from the larder, his behaviour constituted a hindrance to the integrity of the group.

(c) *Leaders and followers:* Much of the writing about leadership tends to be concerned with the way leaders arise in group situations, exercise the functions of planning, decision-making or co-ordinating, and the way acts of leadership contribute to group performance. Traditionally leadership has been conceived of as the exercise of power which is customarily seen as the ability to influence intentionally the behaviour of others. Verba (1967) discusses 'emergent' leaders as opposed to 'legitimate' leaders. He states that the characteristics which are essential in achieving leadership are not necessarily consonant with those characteristics which are needed to maintain a leadership role. A more valuable distinction of two main categories of leadership functions has been made by Lippitt and Seashore (1970): those required to meet the needs at the task level and those required to meet the needs at the group maintenance level. Task functions 'are to facilitate and to co-ordinate group effort in the selection or definition of a common problem and in the solution of that problem', whereas maintenance functions describe 'leadership activities necessary to alter or maintain the way in which members of the group work together, developing loyalty to one another and to the group as a whole'.

Some studies are concerned to show that the task leader and the maintenance leader are not necessarily exclusive kinds of leadership, but that each is more effective in certain situations than the other. The first leader is task-oriented, holding members to the job in hand constantly reminding them of their essential purpose. The second leader is the effective leader who is concerned with the smoothing of relationships within the group. There are several examples of individuals exercising leadership functions in the group homes, only two of which, however, correspond closely to the above set categories. Both of these are significant in terms of the strength of their influence on group behaviour.

At GH3 Gladys Smallfield ensured the residents' limited dependence on outside support and during one period in particular enabled them to cope totally on their own. She collected weekly amounts from each of them and made appropriate budgeting arrangements for the purposes of purchasing household items and paying bills. She gave the other advice, support and assistance when needed, worked hard in the home with both basic housework and in endeavouring to maintain harmonious relationships within the group. She was a 'mother' figure but more accurately a 'leader' figure: she evoked a 'follower' response; was respected by other residents and in the case of Beattie, the least able member of the group, provided a source of reassurance in most of her daily activities. Her patience, goodwill and tenacity were extremely valuable in the home. She unremittingly responded to Beattie's irritating questions that frequently were repeated, and confirmed and disconfirmed her remarks as appropriate. Beattie would also interrupt a conversation to ask Gladys something and she would normally reply sympathetically, 'I've got meself a new dressing gown, haven't I Gladys, tell him, tell him'. Similarly she provided comfort to Ronnie who was prone to become temporarily anxious and depressed for different reasons. Ronnie would expect his girlfriend to visit on certain days and would become disappointed if she did not arrive. He would withdraw into himself if he was worried over something, for example, the ill-health of his cherished dog or his radio not functioning. Despite her obvious superiority in competence, Gladys never dominated the other residents.

The argument that a leader figure existed at GH2 was not so convincing yet it did seem to be the case that John Rylands, husband of Violet, served the kind of maintenance function in the home that has been described as a type of leadership. John was a very easy-going, friendly character. Probably his most valuable attribute was fairness and integrity which he would strive to bring to bear in difficult situations. He would never unduly take sides with his wife when he thought her in the wrong, though on the other hand he could offer her great comfort when she became distressed. As the only male member of the home, he was handled by the others with a rather distant respect as they each vied for his esteem. He was neither moody nor devious and always responded with gratitude to any kindness accorded him. The strength of his leadership lay in the fact that he was capable of bringing stability to emotive and distraught situations involving other group members.

Other residents within the six group homes could be described as occupying leadership roles insofar as they appeared more capable or hard-working than other group members. Barbara Anson at GH1 was hardworking and reliable; Doris Lampton at GH2 was probably more conscientious than any of the others; both Doreen Brampton and Lily Nichols from GH4 and 5 respectively were domineering but hardworking with it. In each of these cases the contributions they made to the homes were acknowledged and usually respected by the others and hence any of them may have achieved a type of leader status. During the Social Workers' strike, Barbara Anson took responsibility for collecting weekly payments from residents and paying these in to the Assessments Section of the Social Services Department. As budgeter, she applied a conscious eye to the way money was spent in the home. As has been said, she would criticise what she considered misuse of resources, like, for example, the electric fire or strive to make saving where possible, such as her suggestion that residents had a cold meal at night on the grounds that the majority if not all of them ate a hot meal at lunchtime. Doris Lampton, with considerable perseverence, had managed to decorate both her own bedroom and the bathroom. She contributed to the upkeep of the garden and was always actively engaged in one pursuit or another. She would cook, clean, sew and, admittedly, try to order people around, but her overall contribution was no less than significant, such that it was impossible not to conclude that without her the other residents would have required extra practical support. Douglas (op. cit.) states that, 'Within any group there will be people who possess resources, abilities, knowledge, skill, which is of value to the group at certain times in its existence. In this sense everyone in the group is a resource person in that he contributes what he has to the group's existence. But certain people have resources not widely distributed. When these resources are required these people become of special value to the group, are invested with 'specialist' power and may assume a temporary leadership role......'

(d) *Mothering:* It is suggested that the individuals described above had a form of high social status in their respective groups. The concept of the 'mother' figure has already once been referred to and its importance is reinforced when further examples appear. To take the case of GH4, Doreen Brampton could be seen as a 'mother' figure in the group, admittedly she was a rather domineering character but at the same time conscientious and eager to ensure that the group home proved capable of managing without outside support. She guided the others and sought to provide them with the support they needed for continuing to live in these circumstances. She was a persuasive character and could convince them that what she was doing was beneficial to them and protective of their interests.

At GH2 Beryl was handled by the others as the 'baby of the family'; she was unable to do many things for herself — cook, shop, use public transport — without assistance. On a joint basis the others would organise her life and tell her what she was and was not permitted to do. Doris Lampton and John, in particular, would occasionally 'pull her leg' and rile her. This however was done in harmless fun and underneath it all, they would genuinely seek to protect her interests albeit at the expense of often appearing over-bearing. The group treated Beryl as their 'child'; they asked her how she had got on 'at school' everyday, said she looked nice in her new coat, told her off when they thought it necessary and instructed her on how to be polite. When Beryl went off on a day-trip organised by the training centre, one group member would arrange to pack her sandwiches and prepare her flask whereas others would deliver instructions: 'Now don't do......', "make sure you're back safely".'

(e) *Sub-groups:* 'A group which is too large for its purpose and organisation pushes certain members out to the periphery and denies them access to the lines of communication and control. This creates a situation favourable to the formation of dissident sub-groups which may become the focus of rebellion and of bids for power' (Northen (1969)). Whereas it would be false to suggest that the total implications of this statement applied to the group homes, there was evidence illustrating the existence of sub-group formations, although these tended to be based on shared interests and the need for companionship. When mentally handicapped people are placed to live in the community with less outside support than they are used to, they naturally expect to become more dependent on their personal resources and hence their need for close and intimate relationships becomes evident. Living in close physical proximity to other individuals demands much from a person in terms of his private self. Some are capable of accepting this challenge and mixing unselfconsciously in a group, whereas others need the protection of at least one one-to-one relationship. Hence sub-groups can evolve neither as a defence against anonymity nor as a bid for leadership, but as a means of providing a mode of expression for certain individuals who need the security of a more private relationship or experience a natural need for companionship.

At GH4 Shirley and Ruth shared a close relationship, attending social events together and confiding in one another in a rather exclusive way. They would come in from work together having usually met from their respective training centres in order to do some shopping. On most Saturdays, they would go 'window gazing' in town, probably dropping into a cafe for a cup of tea. At weekends they would visit the hostel where they had lived previously to see the officer-in-charge and one or two of the residents. At home they would often sit together either leaning against each other, or with their arms around each other. Ruth, who on her arrival in the home had been rathe shy and diffident, gradually became more outgoing, chatty and willing to stand her ground in discussion. She had had a close friend at the hostel and her earlier reticent mood may have been attributable to being separated from this person. Needless to say her growing relationship with Shirley had helped to build up her confidence. Another aspect of this relationship concerned its compatibility with that of the other resident, Doreen, and her boyfriend, John. Doreen would incessantly be discussing the latest saga of this relationship with her co-residents and given that John was a frequent visitor to the home she would enjoy having her opinions on this relationship endorsed by them. They would consistently support, either verbally or otherwise, the continuation of Doreen's relationship, and by doing so help to ensure the exclusiveness of their own.

This type of close one-to-one relationship did not exist to the same extent elsewhere, although the female members of GH3 constituted a sub-group in the sense that many of their activities were shared. They oganised the running of the home and attended social events together. They formed the 'heart of the group' as its integrity seemed to rest on their resourcefulness. They were not in conflict with the two male residents for it could have been interpreted that both 'groups' needed one another equally. The women obtained satisfaction from playing the role of housekeeper to the two men, whilst at the same time criticising their behaviour. This sub-group however, was a form of partnership whereby each of its members frequently required feedback from the others in order to accomplish a task successfully: 'I've done it well, haven't I?'

Lastly, a further type of sub-group existed at GH5 involving three of the residents and was based on the shared leisure interest of visiting a local social club and pub. Whereas Mary, Beattie and Audrey on most evenings went out together, Maud was inclined to stay at home either taking a nap or listening to the radio and Lily occasionally went out alone to another social club. This sub-group did not involve a personal relationship as close and exclusive as that found at GH4 nor did it incorporate such an active working partnership as in GH3. The residents at GH5 received more outside practical support than the others — the Home Helps did the bulk of the shipping, prepared several of the meals, and saw that the house was kept clean. As a result, the residents showed far less initiative in doing things for themselves. There were some indications that, as a group, they functioned at a lower level than most other residents owing to their relatively long period of hos-pitalisation and the resultant apathy and inertia that this experience had induced in them. It is not possible to be too generalistic, however, on this as other residents with a comparable background, for example, at GH3, had succeeded in managing their home with far less dependence on outside support. Accordingly, residents at GH5 interacted less and hence organised their activities together less than some of those elsewhere. They were not a very resourceful group so that even the most

55

minor organised activity such as going out together on a social event appeared striking. One possible interpretation was that this sub-group activity occurred as a response to the dominating influence in the home of Lily and Maud and was a means of avoiding some of the pressures that arose within the group.

(f) *Difficult behaviour:* Some examples of individual difficult behaviour have already been referred to and their importance has been stressed in terms of their implications for the integrity of the groups as a whole. The most significant ones concerned Barbara Turnsnip (GH17 and Doris Grantham (GH2). At GH1 Barbara Turnsnip's behaviour was at times very destructive; she would 'tell stories' about other residents and try to manipulate them into doing things that were not justified. For a long period of time she refused to go to work at the industrial training unit and would insist on remaining in bed all day, not eating and not taking part in any activity. This caused considerable distress and resentment among the others, and at times the matter required the intervention of the support worker. 'She's always in bed, always ill......she hasn't troubled to contact work nor get a doctor. I mean none of us like getting up in the morning, do we?......She's supposed to have a cough, we bring her meals up, but she looks alright, just cough when we ask how she is'. Doris, in particular, became angry on occasions, feeling on the one hand that she must stay at home and support Barbara and on the other that she resented her behaviour deeply and that she had no right to make such demands on the others. This series of incidents revealed as much about the attitudes of other residents as it did about the personality of Barbara. Doris and Barbara Anson took advantage of the opportunity to express themselves on several topics that concerned them, for example, laziness and the importance of taking one's share of the workload.

Another example concerned the deviant and disruptive behaviour of Doris Grantham at GH2. Despite her normally sociable disposition, she was often accused by the two older female residents of being lazy and not taking her turn. Whilst there had been complaints of her behaviour in this way, at the same time the others distrusted her working in the kitchen and were prompt to criticise some of her efforts. This was not as serious however as the more disruptive behaviour that she was inclined to show later on. Having been at the home for almost a year, Doris began to show temper tantrums and aggression in relating to other residents. This behaviour was sporadic but enough to alarm and cause anxiety. For example, Doris Lampton had told her one morning that she had left a light on in the dining room overnight whereupon she 'blew up' immediately and insisted that the others were always 'getting at her'. There were further instances of unpredictable behaviour: 'It's got to the point that we're frightened of saying things to her', (Violet).

The position of Doris Grantham in the group home remained unsettled for whereas, from time to time, problems had arisen regarding the effect of her behaviour on the others, at other times she appeared to mix well.

There is a point beyond which difficult behaviour on the part of an individual of the sort described cannot be adequately contained within a group home. In both above instances the intervention of support workers was needed to try and resolve the situation. There were other examples of individuals exhibiting behaviour different from the general norms of their groups that did not pose such a threat to the harmony, such as George Maybury and Sylvia Beck. Individual resident behaviour only became a 'problem' when its effects were disruptive to the group as a whole and when it appeared unresolvable even with outside support.

A clear example of the latter was the case of GH6 during the time when two residents, Henry and Ian, were living there together. Personality-wise, they were incompatible; Henry was not able to socialise easily, had few interests and could do little for himself in the way of housekeeping. Ian had a demanding, obsessional personality, was not interested in befriending Henry and resented any outside interference in his own activities. Around the house, he was inconsiderate and lazy, spoke resentfully of Henry and refused to share or participate in events. He was unreliable: the Social Worker arranged for him to work voluntarily at an old people's luncheon club and then at an industrial training unit on a full-time basis but on both occasions he reneged and resisted being 'placed' anywhere. Ian considered himself superior in ability to Henry and resented his being associated with him. Henry disliked Ian's selfish habits of refusing to go out to work, playing his records loudly, hoarding food and interrupting the general tranquillity of his life. At times, Henry could become vicious and lock Ian out or throw things at him — these incidents were rare but they made Ian respond with further aggressive behaviour and resentment and no compromise eventually proved possible. Ian left the home on his own accord, moving to a 'working men's' hostel.

(iv) *Outsiders*

The groups survived with the aid of various kinds of outside support, consisting not only of official support but also that from other types of informal source. The principal visitors to the homes, however, were the official support workers and others from the service agencies. There were in addition people who visited the homes as volunteers and friends but in almost all cases these were related to the official networks of support. They included local volunteers, residential workers and friends of those already providing support in an official capacity.

(a)*Official support workers:* The groups received the help on a visiting basis from Social Workers, Social Work Assistants, Home Helps and in the case of one home, a Nursing Assistant. This help varied in content among homes as did the manner in which the support workers were recognised by individual groups of residents. The support worker provided practical aid in accomplishing tasks, assisted the group in the solution of problems, and provided counselling or the role of a friend to whom individuals could turn.

Practical help — In all cases Home Helps provided practical aid in domestic tasks such as shopping, cooking and cleaning. They advised residents on the right methods to use but the amount of actual teaching they provided differed and was usually no more than of a basic kind. There were examples of assigned projects such as taking a resident along to a supermarket in order to teach him to shop (GH6) and teaching a particular resident to use the washing machine (GH5) but these were isolated cases as, in general, Home Helps tended to act as homemakers, carrying out basic household tasks in addition to socialising with residents to a limited degree. Home Helps at GH2 and 5 mended residents' clothes either in the homes or by taking them home with them and in the first case Home Helps sometimes accompanied residents to buy clothes. The Nursing Assistant at GH3 helped with practical duties over and above the basic ones of shopping and cleaning which the residents managed themselves. Her contribution was in the form of carrying out more complex or strenuous home-based tasks like ironing and putting up curtains, changing plugs or giving the house a thorough clean. Social Work support involved the accomplishment of other practical tasks, including managing residents' finances and providing the means for residents to develop outside social contacts. There were cases where a Social Worker had introduced residents to local clubs and societies, had arranged transport for them and had escorted them to see the GP, chiropodist or optician.

Advice — Support workers offered advice to residents on how to carry out tasks, whom to contact in given situations and how to deal with tradesmen, neighbours and shopkeepers. Redl (1942), in writing on group work, introduced the idea of a 'Central Person' being a form of leadership based on common emotional responses to one person. In group work the very nature of the professional group worker's situation, coupled with the needs and expectations of the members of the group, creates a common relationship of all the members to the group worker. This common response existed in some group homes towards certain individual support workers. Residents looked to the support worker for help and advice. At GH1 the Social Work Assistant gave advice to the group on how to manage the home and organise housework, make friendly approaches to neighbours and deal with door-to-door trades-peoples. At GH2 the Social Work Assistant

58

organised annual holidays for residents at different boarding-houses and advised them on how to conduct themselves. In addition, advice was given on practical problems: how to arrange their day and whom to contact if they needed immediate advice or supervision. Residents approached the support person if they needed advice on a personal matter, for example, if they had been invited to a social function by a work colleague and did not wish to go or if they had a physical ailment which they felt needed attention.

Problem-solving — Usually the Social Worker or Social Work Assistant involved in each home took the overall role of being a problem-solver for the residents. In addition to offering advice to individuals, her main contribution was in dealing with problems that affected the group as a whole. Some of these were of a practical kind, like ensuring that the group had an adequate supply of bread in the event of a local manu-facturers' strike or contacting the Housing Department to deal with structural repairs or the TV rental agent to repair a set. Others were more complex concerning the interpersonal relations of residents. In the event of a disagreement, the usual approach taken was for the support worker to first allow individuals to voice openly their complaints or criticisms of one another and then to try and encourage them to become understanding and tolerant of one another's ways. Notes taken recording a particular incident in one of the homes revealed the support worker in the role of group counsellor:

'. . . . . . She asked all five (residents) to attend a meeting and then threw out the two complaints she had had to the relevant parties involved for discussion'.

A.   'Sylvia, you've a problem haven't you?'

'She (pointing to Doris) has been telling me I can't wash my clothes at night. When I came in late she was getting ready for bed and she told me I couldn't wash my clothes'. Doris denied this. (Support worker) intervened, saying that Doris was probably only joking.

B.   'Barbara, what's your problem?' (to Barbara Turnsnip)

'She (pointing to Doris) keeps picking on me'. Doris denied the accusation. Barbara Turnsnip repeated that Doris kept "getting at" her. Doris received support from Barbara Anson who said that they were "fed up" with Barbara Turnsnip as she stayed in bed, refusing to go to work and did not play her part in household jobs, also she refused to eat. This antisocial attitude had annoyed them. Doris partly agreed with this but did not, however, say that she had "been at" Barbara Turnsnip to get up and go to work. Brenda remained silent throughout, but when asked to offer a view, nodded in agreement that Barbara Turnsnip was doing all these things. Doris went on to say that Barbara Turnsnip had been criticising her (probably as a result of being "got at" by Doris), particularly her cooking. Barbara Turnsnip denied this although adding, "but you must admit there are some things you cannot do Doris".

None of the group tended to show much sign of an ability to empathise or

59

reconcile their differences, whereas (the support worker) was very diplomatic and prevented actual emotional outbursts. She strove to balance the various interests involved, treating each resident as an individual and telling them, "you've got to learn to accept one another, to accept one another's foibles and bad points".'

In another home the Social Work Assistant took a key role in solving group problems simply by doing most of the planning and thinking for the residents. She organised social events, shopping for specific items and their attendance at clinics, surgeries, day centres and an evening class. Her approach to them was on the following lines: 'Now look at it this way, I'm not telling you to do this or do that, I'm just saying this, but it's up to you to decide for yourself'. She made suggestions to individual residents to follow a course of action and proceeded to set up appropriate arrangements whereby any problem met on the way would be dealt with.

A further example of problem-solving concerned those cases where a support worker had been pressurised to intervene in a group situation either by another support worker or the residents themselves. At GH2 the Social Work Assistant was a 'central' figure in the support team to whom both Home Helps were, for most practical purposes, accountable. When residents had a problem they either told the Home Helps or the Social Work Assistant and, by and large, when the Home Helps had a problem, of whatever kind, they told the Social Work Assistant. Minor problem situations of this kind arose frequently at GH2. An example concerned the incident of a 'mystery visitor' received by Violet Rylands. Violet had furtively admitted into the home a man whom she had proceeded to converse with 'behind closed doors', intentionally excluding the other residents. Much to the annoyance of both the other residents and the Home Helps she had refused to divulge the man's business with her other than to state that he was known by her son Jeffrey (her first illegitimate son who was married and living nearby). The Social Work Assistant felt obliged to interrogate Violet on this matter on the formal grounds that the Department had an official responsibility for the welfare of residents and that this included taking steps to prevent exploitation. She spoke to Violet in the company of the others and explained to her that although she did not wish to pry into her personal affairs she needed all the same to know whom she was dealing with and what, if anything, she was committing herself to. The Home Help was very intrigued by these goings-on and adamant to have revealed to her the true facts. The outcome was that Violet admitted she was being persuaded by her son to take out an insurance policy from which he was to benefit in the event of her death.

Friendship — Support staff at the direct care level acted as friends to residents in addition to performing their more official functions.

Friendship meant taking an extra interest in the group as individuals; it meant experiencing things with as well as doing things for them. Being a friend implies a relationship built on mutual trust and liking and the close relationships that evolved reflected the presence of close patterns of personal interaction that became the foundation on which many developments were based. The evidence for the existence of friendly relations between support workers and residents came in various forms. Sometimes they would go for an evening out together. However, to take an example from GH1, this type of 'socialising' was not always the result of a personal relationship between individuals. Social work staff took the group for 'a drink' in a nearby pub on one evening; on another a Home Help accompanied by her husband took them out somewhere else. This more 'organised' activity where one party would be seen as taking the other out somewhere contrasted with the type of event where one or more residents invited the Social Work Assistant to accompany them in the normal way to a dance or to have a meal.

Support workers gave away personal possessions. One Social worker brought to the home a suitcase full of dresses which she had outgrown to be used by one of the residents. Other household items including food were sometimes handed over if someone saw a need or wished to make a gift. One Home Help received a mail order catalogue for the purchase of a wide range of domestic and personal items. She invited the residents to make weekly payments to obtain chosen items and sometimes paid their dues for them in return for their helping her with her own housework.

Friendship was manifested in the way residents felt at ease in 'calling in' at the home of a support worker whether for a specific reason or simply for a chat. This applied to those who resided in the same local neighbourhood and was reciprocated by the frequent visits the support worker made to the group home. Such support workers 'popped in' to the home at random whether or not they were meant to be officially working there. Friendship was shown, in several instances, in the manner by which residents and staff related to one another — they would joke together, give one another parting kisses and show genuine affection and consideration in their conversation. There was ample evidence to show that this sort of relationship existed particularly involving the female residents.

(b) *Unofficial support:* There were several examples of 'unofficial' support but the majority had in common the fact that they consisted of individuals who were related in some way to the existing official support network. GH1 received regular weekly visits from two different married couple volunteers, one of them associated with the local church. These were social visits but practical help was also offered. A domestic science teacher employed by the Social Services Department arranged to visit both GH1 and 4 in the evening on an alternative fortnightly basis. Cookery skills were taught to those residents present and recipes given for making items such as pancakes, 'hotpot' and treacle pudding. In spite of much enthusiasm shown on these occasions the teacher's assessment at the end of the first year of practice was however that 'they' had shown little ability in absorbing her instructions for any length of time. Visits were made to homes by individuals who had been associated with one or more residents in a 'caring' role prior to their transfer to a group home. Occasionally a hospital nurse might 'drop in' if she happened to be in the neighbourhood (GH3 and 5). In GH5 the Social Work Assistant had arranged for a local volunteer to call in the morning to help one resident cross the nearby road to catch her bus for work; she had also arranged for a hairdresser (a friend of her sister) to visit the home once a fortnight to deal with the residents' hair.

(c) *Boyfriends and girlfriends:*   Several residents had a close friend of the opposite sex living outside the home whom they saw and who some- times visited the group home. This normally concerned no more than one resident per group although these relationships sometimes had implications for the behaviour of the other group members. Most commonly relationships were happily encouraged by other residents and the situation was such that the boyfriend/girlfriend visited the home and was welcomed as a friend to the group as a whole. At GH3 Ronnie had a girlfriend called Mabel who lived and worked as a domestic in a private nursing home on the opposite side of the city. She visited the home usually every week, at regular times and Ronnie's 'face would drop' if she did not arrive on schedule. 'The others complained bitterly about his mood while he was upstairs. They said that he'd been moan- ing all morning and taking it out on them just because Mabel hadn't come to see him . . . . . .'

At GH4 the rather dominant influence of Doreen's relationship with John was not easily ignored: John was almost her sole topic of conver- sation; they eventually became engaged and a feud began over whether and where they should live together on a 'trial marriage' basis. John was at the home frequently and it was never clear whether his presence had favourable consequences for the other two female residents. Doreen spoke out strongly to the effect that John was well accepted by the others, who always nodded in agreement, sometimes making what could be taken as favourable remarks such as 'he makes us laugh' and 'we're used to him now'. On one occasion, after it was found that John had stayed at the home for a whole weekend, the others were keen to remark on how helpful John had been in a domestic way: 'he takes in our washing', 'he hoovers about', 'he dries dishes'. Having lived in the group home for almost two and half years Doreen was eventually trans- ferred to a Social Services Department hostel along with John, who had during most of this time been living at home with his mother. The intention was to make an assessment of their capability of living together. During this whole period, however, John developed quite a close relationship with the other two residents, one of whom was often seen shopping or out visiting with the couple.

There were contrasts to this type of accommodating approach of the group towards a member's boy/girlfriend. Some individuals chose to meet up with their partners outside the home with the result that the relationships had no noticeable effects on other group members, but there were other instances where a group (or at least certain members) expressed a clear antipathy towards a resident's partner. There were no seriously bad consequences observed as, for example, with the case at GH1 and Sylvia's boyfriend, Albert, where the effect was simply that the two met up outside the home, visiting it together only on rare occasions. Albert lived in a hostel and worked during the day in a factory 'sweeping up'; the others abhorred his 'bad manners' and rather shabby dress and criticised the way he ate at the table, picking up his food and occasionally dropping it on the floor. As a result Albert ceased coming to the home 'for tea' and instead Sylvia began to visit his hostel more frequently. Their contacts increased and the friendship grew such that Sylvia's other contacts with the group became tenuous. Having been at the home for almost two and a half years, Sylvia eventually moved out to live with Albert in a council property, after which they became married.

(d) *Pets:*   Four out of six groups owned pets — two dogs, two cats and a budgerigar, one group having both dogs. They were bought or found by individual members of the groups, and were well cared for. They provided a means for residents to express their feelings of affection and love and in one particular case the house animals became very central to the daily life of the group. The dogs at GH3 were their 'pride and job', although they were specifically attached to individual residents who doted on them as if they were children. When the conversation halted, attention was turned to the antics of the dogs. Each person spoke to the individual dogs fondly and without inhibition. They played a vital role in contributing to the harmony of the home. Their treatment was as good if not better than that offered to humans — half of anything consumed by an individual went to one of the dogs: a cup of tea, expensive sweets, biscuits. At GH1 Barbara Anson owned a kitten to whom she devoted much care; the others tolerated the animal, and, at best, showed a like-minded affection towards it, yet, at the same time, the kitten became a source of argument between Barbara and another group member who complained that it had been scratching the furniture or that it made the house smell. These were not serious arguments in themselves, however, as they were usually founded on some other issue.

63

In any home a pet can provide companionship and fulfil human needs and the group homes were no exception to this.

(v) *Attitudes and behaviour*

One of the most important characteristics of all the groups lay both in the way the residents presented themselves to other people and in the way they behaved and talked generally. Inevitably their previous experiences had conditioned them into thinking along some rather set lines but also these experiences had instilled in them a fundamental appreciation of their present living circumstances. More than usually they were hospitable and welcoming in their attitude towards strangers and friends in particular, making earnest effort to make a person comfortable in their home, preparing coffee or tea, bringing biscuits and keen to converse. Admittedly, being in the position of an introduced 'friend', they always felt an obligation to the writer in the sense that they most likely saw him as someone prepared to take an interest in them for good reasons. However, many experiences led this writer to believe that these positive expressions of feeling were not unique and that on the whole they were genuinely pleased to welcome visitors into their home.

This show of hospitality may have been a reflection of their desire to present as people exhibiting 'normal' behaviour. It became very noticeable that all bar a few residents strove hard to assert their ability to survive independently in the community, eschewing the need for official support and, what is perhaps more important, they made a conscious effort to ensure that their abilities were recognised by outside people. The residents of GH1, 3 and 4 in particular impressed one by the extent to which they were prepared to take a serious pride in their home and to manage housekeeping efficiently. A conscious attempt, furthermore, to 'deny' their handicap was evident on the part of GH1 residents. For example, their personal manners were very proper; they showed etiquette and politeness in conversation which usually dealt with a range of guarded topics – the 'rush hour', the price of food items, 'what's in the newspapers'. Openly they never appeared to argue, over-talk or behave too affectionately towards one another such as to always preserve a certain dignity in their relationship, at least in the presence of guests. One one occasion a resident described to the others a TV play she had watched the previous evening concerning a group home for the mentally handicapped. She described the story well rather as any lay-person would have done to another, making no references to her being familiar with this 'problem' at all. In responding, the others acted likewise, failing to reveal any signs of identifying with a situation of this sort.

On the other hand, some behaviours of residents indicated 'institutional' habits and experiences to such an extent as to be possibly viewed as constituting a barrier towards adjusting to community living. They were attention-seeking towards outside visitors, talking to them incessantly of their problems and worries and demanding a kind of constant attention that was often not possible in the circumstances. They would sometimes 'fire' questions, demand answers and insist on actions being taken with hardly any consideration to others involved. Similarly, several individuals showed an obsessional tendency to oust one another in 'showing-off' their possessions and accomplishments to visitors. They would repeatedly show, for example, family photographs or presents they had received. The women at GH2 and 3 brought down from their rooms articles of clothing that they had acquired — dresses, shoes, hats — and displayed them for approval.

The behaviour of residents at GH5 often reflected their long 'institutional' history — they sat in their chairs fidgeting, contorting their faces or staring vacantly. At mealtimes they ate with their mouths full — on one occasion eating cold toast and corned beef overpowered with tomato sauce with little, if any, awareness of sharing the table with others. There was rarely any verbal communication among them and from time to time individuals would mumble things to themselves not prompting any response from the other residents. There were often instances where it was noticed that the past experiences of residents had a bearing on their behaviour, examples being an apparent indifference to a need for personalised clothing — 'Have you enough trousers, John?' 'Ay, I think I've enough......I forget what colour they are......Any'll do,' or an almost obsessional tendency to routinise behaviour as in the case of the 'cook' at GH3 — 'On every occasion Bertha is cooking something; she never sits down for more than a minute without jumping up 'to look at the pots' in the kitchen, 'to get the dinner on', 'to get the tea on', 'to see if the potatoes are done', and so on. It's a persistent 24 hour chore......George's breakfast, the group's breakfast, the group's dinner, George's dinner, the group's tea......'

(vi) *Summary*

The long-term participation in and observation of group home based activities provided considerable information and insights into the personalities of individual residents and the relative abilities of the groups to live harmoniously together. There was evidence of residents' working closely together organising their homes in a constructive way, helping one another in a practical way and planning activities together. Household tasks had been shared: 'role taking' and 'rota' systems had been evident in some cases but usually a more flexible system had emerged from experience, suggesting that both methods of organisation had their limitations in practice. The shared past experiences of some residents had most probably contributed towards mutual understandings, like-minded attitudes and behaviour, and close friendships. Additionally they shared a desire to make a success of their opportunity to live together outside a more supervised residential setting.

Whereas there existed factors more evidently conducive to the harmony of the groups, they were characterised also by internal divisions among members that often were seen to have serious implications for their ability to survive intact. Conflict between residents was commonplace but usually founded on only minor issues; other antagonisms arose that required the helpful intervention of a support worker but these were rarely sufficiently serious as to render the integrity of the home vulnerable. However, there were further conflicts between specific individuals that gave rise to stressful situations and that were not so clearly resolvable.

Some residents were seen in the role of 'leader' or 'scapegoat' in their respective group and, in some cases, these had positive implications for the maintenance of group harmony. The fact that an individual was able to take on the responsibility of leading the group in some way lessened the need for outside support along with enhancing the morale and status of the individuals concerned. The factors surrounding the process of 'scapegoating' are more complex to interpret as they imply the maintenance of a group's stability at the expense of an individual member. The examples discussed did not have serious results as they would have done in cases involving genuine victimisation, although they did show a hardening of attitudes on the part of residents towards particular members which needed the involvement of an outsider to 'defuse' the situation.

'Mothering' relationships, and 'sub-group' friendships were also shown to exist. In each case they fulfilled natural human needs for affection and companionship. Mothering was based on a desire for the handicapped person to assert an ability to care for someone else rather than being the recipient of care from another sources, as was usually the case. It proved that individuals of low practical ability were able to live in these circumstances, dependent more on one or more residents rather than on the 'official' support available. It would have been inaccurate to perceive sub-group friendships as deriving from a feeling of individual isolation within a group, as instead these tended to be based on shared interests and ideas. Although potentially divisive to group interests, the evidence suggests more of a compatibility with the remaining members of the group. The difficult behaviour of certain individuals constituted, however, a more serious threat to group stability. Expressions of disruptive resident behaviour required the support worker to intervene but residual problems usually existed and particular ones emerged as 'long term'.

There were several components to the role of 'official' support workers — that of practical helper, adviser, problem-solver and friend — although the emphasis on each differed depending on the person and the situation. Similarly different overall approaches were employed by support workers in carrying out their role and these had consequences both for their relationships with other workers and the attitudes of the residents themselves. There was, in addition, a range of 'unofficial' support provided but the majority of this was either organised by or associated with the 'official' support network. In terms of 'unofficial' support there was a marked absence of residents' relatives, ordinary members of the neighbourhood and friends, apart from girl/boy friends of the opposite sex of a small number of individual residents. The usual response from the rest of the group was to be accommodating towards an individual's girl/boy friend but there was at least one example when this was not the case. Some homes possessed pets which were devotedly cared for, though they were usually the responsibility of a particular resident.

Finally, certain overall trends were observable in the behaviour of residents insofar as they had implications for the manner in which they presented themselves to outsiders and in other social situations. The influence of 'institutional' experiences was felt sometimes in the way they conducted themselves — seeking the attention of others, 'showing off' their possessions and withdrawing into their 'own world'; whereas, in contrast, other types of behaviour illustrated the extent to which they had desired to present as 'normal' — their topics of conversation, their ways of relating to each other, their self-assertion.

SECTION 4

Residents' Views on Contacts and Support

(i) *Introduction*

One of the general principles of the Government White Paper (1971) was that 'Mentally handicapped children and adults should not be segregated unnecessarily from other people of similar age nor from the general life of the local community'. These ideas were endorsed in the Sheffield Feasibility Study Report (1971) which proposed (p.iii) 'a full range of services for the mentally handicapped should be developed with the object of enabling the mentally handicapped person to live as much a part of the community as his disabilities allow......' and (p.5) 'The needs of the mentally handicapped person and his family are not fundamentally different from the requirements of the rest of the community......segregation of this group of people by provision of an entirely separate service is undesirable'. The experience of mentally handicapped people living in the community, their attitudes and those of community members towards them constitute an important source of data in the evaluation of community-based units. Whereas there appears to be much current interest in these areas, little substantial research data are available upon which future planning decisions can be made. What there is largely consists of data on the attitudes of neighbours and local people to both hostels and group homes and those residing in them and rarely, for example, (Lundblad and Viktor (1975)), that which encompasses the views of residents themselves towards community living.

The attitude of the community towards mentally handicapped people is an important factor in the success of a small unit in the community. Davis (1977) found that sympathetic neighbours play an important part in helping to foster local links. Malin and Race (1978) and Tyne (1978) have indicated the differing opinions on whether the community should be encouraged to interact with 'the unit' (open days, use of facilities for meetings, and so on) or whether individual residents should be encouraged to go out into the community and foster personal attachments. Grunewald and Thor (1978) outline three parts to integration: physical (placing of the unit in the community); functional (residents use community services) and social (becoming an accepted member of the society).

Resistance from some residents is often evident in the siting of new accommodation for mentally handicapped people, (Nelson (1978)) and yet policies of community care assume that attitudes towards the mentally handicapped are such that siting facilities in the community will encourage care BY the community as opposed to care merely IN the community. Various factors relating to people's acceptance of a new group home for mentally handicapped adults have been studied, (Sigelman (1976)). More favourable attitudes to mentally handicapped people were expressed by the young and middle-aged compared to older people; by blacks and self-styled liberals and by people who rented rather than owned their homes. Sigelman pointed out that these expressed attitudes do not necessarily mean acceptance in practice, and she suggests that, since informing local people can lead to organised opposition, it is better to say nothing until the place is opened. This 'low profile' entrance can be contrasted, (Weber (1978)) with the 'high profile' entrance, educating anyone who will have contact with the new home, involving a planned, intensive, rapidly executed educational effort. Weber discusses a large number of factors which have been found, by experience and observation, to relate to acceptance of group homes for a variety of clients. High resistance might be expected, for instance, from attractive, neat neighbourhoods comprising mainly single family households and from areas where there may be other group homes that may be fearful of their being a 'human service ghetto'.

Little literature exists on community acceptance or opposition to new hostels for the mentally handicapped. However, one recent study in

London, (Locker et. al. (1978)) did not find widespread opposition to the hostel; 60 per cent of their sample were more favourable than opposed. Another study of units in Sheffield, (Dalgleish (1979)) endorsed these sentiments, summarising that 'It appeared that the more a unit resembled local housing, the better it was liked. Unusual design features occasionally led local residents to reason that mentally handicapped people must *need* 'special' housing'. People with an inadequate understanding of mental handicap were more likely to feel negatively about the hostel. Pushkin (1976) found two-thirds of the people she talked to did not know what the term 'mentally subnormal' meant but no socio-demographic variable was found to be associated with expressed attitude towards the hostel. Providing more information about mental handicap then would, they concluded, result in more people reacting favourably to the hostel.

The present study is concerned with group home residents' views of their contacts with relatives, neighbours, friends and service agencies. It is concerned with establishing the value and extent of these contacts as seen through the eyes of residents. The method was through a semi-structured interview (Appendix B) with all residents which was taperecorded. A preliminary interview schedule was used with four residents from another group home. This was modified only slightly for the purpose of the main study.

(ii) *Findings*

(a) Contact with relatives: The overall number of relatives mentioned by the 24 residents totaled 97*, averaging 4 per resident. Seven residents stated that they had 6 or more living relatives and 6 had 2 or less. Residents were asked to name the relatives with whom they had contact — whether face-to-face contact or by other means, for example, by telephone or mail. Altogether 55* relatives were mentioned with whom residents had face-to-face contact, averaging 2.3 per resident. Five residents, however, had no contacts either face-to-face or by other means — 3 of these residents were from the same home (GH5) and 4 of them had already stated that they had relatives. Fifteen residents stated that they had one or more relatives with whom they had no contacts. There was a variation in the extent of face-to-face contacts both between residents and between homes. (See table, top next page.)

Of the many relatives mentioned with whom residents had face-to-face contact, brothers and sisters were the most common — 17 out of 24 residents said they 'saw' one or more. No resident stated that he/she had a mother, although two said they had a father and that they were in

---

* Husbands/wives and children of the said relatives were often mentioned but were *not* included if they lived in the same house.

Home	Average number of face-to-face contacts per resident
GH1	2.2
GH2	3.4
GH3	2.8
GH4	2.0
GH5	0.8
GH6	3.0

contact. Ten residents stated that they 'heard from' one or more of their relatives — usually no more than 3 although one stated that she 'heard from' five. Residents were asked to describe the frequency with which face-to-face contacts took place. They were not asked to stipulate the circumstances of meetings, whether, for example, they occurred through home visits or by chance, though it appeared that the majority were through visits made by residents to relatives' homes — 4 residents, however, stated that they had one or more of their relatives visit them in the group home but this was only an indication. It was difficult to be exact regarding the frequency of meetings as answers were usually expressed in imprecise terms, for example, 'not much', 'sometimes', 'occasionally', 'most weeks usually'. However, it was possible to divide up such answers into the three following categories:

	Number of face-to-face contacts of total resident group
1. 'weekly' (includes 'frequently', 'a lot', 'most weeks', and other similar terms)	19 (+ 1 fortnightly) = 20
2. 'monthly' or thereabouts	4
3. Others, referred to as 'less frequently', 'occasionally', 'not much', 'once or twice a year' and similar terms	31
Total	55

Breaking down the above scores for each home presented the following pattern with GH1 having, proportionate to other types of contact, the most 'weekly' face-to-fact contacts with relatives:

	Categories 1	2	3	Sub-total
GH1	5	1	5	11
GH2	7	0	10	17
GH3	5	2	7	14
GH4	1	0	5	6
GH5	1	1	2	4
GH6	1	0	2	3
			Total	55

Looking more closely at the 'weekly' contacts of each home with respect to individual residents, it was found, for example, that 10 out of the 15 residents living at GH1, 2 and 3 had one or more 'weekly' contacts and that two of these residents had no less than 3 'weekly' contacts with relatives. (In both cases the relatives were either brothers or sisters).

Residents were asked how they spent their time with the relative with whom they came into contact, what 'help' they received from them and whether they helped them in return. In most cases they said they would 'just sit and talk' or 'go for tea', although occasionally mention was made of their accompanying a relative to the shops or on a walk. In describing 'help' they received, the majority of residents stated 'not much' (or something similar) — including sometimes expressions such as 'she would do (if I asked her)' of 'She can't (through some disability)'. Some mentioned 'help' that they received but this was often phrased in fairly unspecified terms: 9 residents said that they received money and/or gifts of one kind or another, 6 said that they received a meal, usually a tea, and 3 said that they received 'help' which for the present purpose could be described as advice and/or information. Thirteen residents stated that they gave 'help' to one or more of their relatives; this was usually in the form of performing simple household jobs, for example, washing-up or going on errands.

Illustrations — It was difficult to obtain precise answers to several of the questions asked, partly due to the poor memory of some residents and to the problems they experienced in describing activities and responding to direct questions. In addition it could be concluded that a less structured interview was needed that would have encouraged residents to speak more freely of their contacts with relatives in the more general sense rather than one that concentrated on very specific items. This factor has important implications for the quality of the data obtained. The following is a recording of a typical interview on the subject of contact with relatives and is illustrative of these points.

Q (Question)
A (Answer)

Q 'What relatives have you got?
   A Only one brother dead.
Q You've got a brother?
   A No I got two brothers.
Q Anyone else?
   A I got one sister no two sisters and a sister-in-law oh course there's

71

two sisters-in-law I've got two brothers.

Q What are your brothers' names?
A Georgie and Harry.

Q Sisters-in-law, what are their names?
A I got one sister-in-law that's no relation to me now well she is with my young nephew you know.

Q You don't know the names of the two sisters-in-law?
A Yes I do.

Q What are they called?
A Ayleen, Joyce and this one that was to my dead brother that's Evelyn.

Q What are the names of your two sisters?
A Nellie and Edna.

Q Which of them do you see, do you see George?
A Yes I do.

Q Do you hear from him, does he write to you?
A No.

Q Do you see Harry?
A I saw him last . . . . . .

Q Do you hear from him, does he write to you?
A Yes he wrote me a lovely letter.

Q What about Nellie, do you see her?
A No I don't see her at all. Not unless I go down.

Q Do you hear from Nellie?
A No.

Q What about Edna, do you see her?
A No.

Q Do you hear from her?
A No.

Q What about Ayleen, do you see her?
A Yes, see her every week.

Q Do you hear from Ayleen, does she write to you?
A Well, she hasn't wrote to me lately.

Q What about Joyce, do you hear from her?
A Yes I do.

Q Do you see her?
A I don't see her until I go down to Spalding to see her.

Q So you just see her sometimes?
A Yes.

Q How often do you see George?
A Every week.

Q How often do you see Harry?
A You can't tell 'cause I don't know when he's going to fetch me over or what, sometimes every few months.

Q How often does he write to you, Harry?

A   About once a week.

Q   Nellie and Edna, you don't hear from at all?
A   No.

Q   How often do you see Ayleen?
A   Every week.

Q   How often do you see Joyce?
A   Well, she's same as Harry.

Q   When did you last see George?
A   On Saturday.

Q   When was the time before that?
A   Week before.

Q   What do you do when you see George?
A   I just kiss him and. . . . . .

Q   Do you just talk to him?
A   Yes.

Q   Do you go out with him at all?
A   No.

Q   What help do you get from George?
A   Well, none really.

Q   He doesn't help you?
A   No.

Q   Money help?
A   No.

Q   Presents?
A   Oh he might send me a Christmas present.

Q   Do you help George?
A   Yes, I help wash all pots and that.

Q   When did you last see Harry?
A   It was first week in July.

Q   When was the time before that, do you remember?
A   No.

Q   What do you do when you see Harry?
A   I give him a hug. . . . . .

Q   Just sit and talk to him or do you go out with him?
A   Oh, I go out with him.

Q   Go out for a walk or to town or something?
A   I go to Spalding town and we went to biggest lake side that there
    is.

Q   What help do you get from Harry, does he help you at all?
A   He sometimes gives me presents.

Q   He doesn't help you in any other way?
A   No.

Q   Do you help him?
A   Well, I can't can I?

Q   What about Ayleen, when was the last time you saw her?

A   Saturday.
Q   When was the time before that?
A   The week before.
Q   What do you do when you see Ayleen, how do you spend your time with her?
A   Just spend same as I do with George. Just talk.
Q   What help do you get from Ayleen?
A   I get a bit of help you know with going to shops for her.
Q   That's you helping her, isn't it? What does she do for you?
A   She gives me what I fetch and she gives me anything.
Q   What does she give you?
A   Sometimes she gives me some money.
Q   Anything else?
A   No.
Q   Do you help her?
A   Well, no I don't.
Q   What about Joyce, when was the last time you saw her, July was it?
A   Yes.
Q   When was the time before that?
A   Don't know.
Q   What do you do when you see Joyce?
A   Kiss her and......
Q   Do you go out with her?
A   Yes.
Q   What do you do with her?
A   I go out with her in motor car.
Q   Does she help you at all, Joyce?
A   She does when......we sit and laugh and if I tell her anything you know just move my hands like that and she has me in fits.
Q   She makes you laugh?
A   Yes.
Q   Do you help her?
A   No, not much?'

Describing both whether 'help' was given and the kind that it was at times posed a difficult task resulting in confusion on the part of the interviewee and a tendency for him/her to stray from the point or else to give answers that could not be 'classified' in any precise way.

Q   'Does he help you at all?
A   No, he helps his mother do all the housework and all paper you know all housework.
Q   He doesn't help you in any way?
A   No.
Q   Doesn't he give you anything?

74

A   He might give me one or two cigarettes.
Q   Cigarettes?
A   Yes but I give it him back.
Q   Do you help him at all?
A   I don't, he can help himself at 25, he should help me'.

Futhermore, residents expressed views on their relatives which were not directly sought but nonetheless were of interest in understanding the nature of any contacts they had.

Example (1)
(Commenting on her brother)

'I'd like to see that one with the boys 'cause I not seen them for a bit, both got good jobs you know, one works on computers and the other one works at the bank and his young lady works at the same place as him and other's a window-dresser'.

Example (2)

Q   'What relatives do you have?
A   No only a stepmoher but I don't have anything to do with her 'cause she shoved me in these places'.

(b) *Contact with neighbours:*   All but three (out of the total group of 24) residents said that they knew one or more neighbours. Leaving aside GH6, in all but one home answers indicated that the same neighbours were known by the majority if not all of the residents, although the actual number mentioned varied among individuals.

To summarise: All at GH1 knew the 'lady next door'; all at GH2 knew Mrs. Ho next door (who was also one of the group's two Home Helps), 4 out of 5 knew either one or two neighbours 'across the road', and one resident stated that she knew 5 neighbours and 'many who I say hello to but (do) not know their names'; 3 at GH3 said they knew either one or two neighbours in their road, the other 2 said they knew no one; all at GH4 said they knew the 'lady next door' and a 'lady across the road'; 3 at GH5 said they knew 'neighbours' who worked in the shops situated opposite the home, one of the other two mentioned someone else; the one resident at GH6 said he knew the 'lady next door'.

From the above it was clear that the majority of residents knew a next door neighbour and in addition approximately half knew either one or two others 'in the road'. There was evidence that a small number 'knew' additional neighbours but did not know their names — 'I say hello to a lot of people'.

	Number of residents	Aggregate total number of neighbours mentioned by individual residents	Actual number of individual neighbours mentioned
GH1	5	5	1
GH2	5	15	6
GH3	5	6	6
GH4	3	7	3
GH5	5	8	5
GH6	1	1	1
	Total 42		22

Is it reasonable to expect that residents belonging to the same home should know the same neighbour? One example where this was not the case was GH3 as each of the three residents who stated that they knew neighbours referred to different people. In contrast, each resident at GH1 stated that they only knew one of the two next door neighbours. Residents were asked to rate their liking of neighbours on a 5-point scale from 'strongly like' to 'strongly dislike' — in the majority of cases answers were rated as being equivalent to 'quite like', although several were rated as 'strongly like' (including all residents at GH2 in reference to their next door neighbour/Home Help). One resident rates a neighbour in terms equivalent to 'quite dislike'.

When residents were asked how often they saw their neighbours to talk to, the majority of replies were stated in terms such as 'not much', 'not often', 'sometimes', 'now and again', or 'most weeks'. There were few instances of frequent contact, illustrated by terms like 'most days', 'everyday', or 'often'. This latter group included the next door neighbours mentioned at GH1, 2 and 4 and also the local shop people in relation to GH5. Contacts, however, differed among the residents of each home such that some admitted to greater contact than others with a particular neighbour. Residents only gave very general approximations of the length of time they spent talking to individual neighbours, though it was possible to broadly distinguish two types of answer: 'a couple of minutes'/ 'not long' and 'for a long time'/'half an hour'/'a long time if she's not busy'. Of the 42 contacts established, 10 fell in the second of these categories. The majority of contacts entailed everyday conversation and were normally chance encounters. Many of these consisted solely of greetings — 'hello, how are you getting on?' 'Alright, thank you'.

In the case of one half of the said contacts of individual residents with respective neighbours, interviewees reported that they received 'help' of one kind or another. More meaningfully, this 'help' was given to one or more residents by 11 neighbours in all. For example, GH1's next door neighbour helped by doing practical jobs — fixing a doorknob, replacing a lightbulb; GH2's next door neighbour gave a wide range of help, for example, gifts, altering/mending clothes, sorting out money; the neighbouring shop people gave GH5 residents practical advice in the use of public facilities, for example, drawing out money from the Post Office, packing items into a bag, how to use the cigarette machine. Yet with the exception of the 'help' given to GH2 residents by their next door neighbour (Mrs. Ho/Home Help), there was overall little 'help' as such given by neighbours. Most 'help' was described in the form of simple advice or instructions, for example, indicating directions, informing of which shops to use, buses to catch or when tradesmen visited. On the assumption that 'help' is often provided on a reciprocal basis, it could be expected that the above 'help' would be returned in some way. There was, however, hardly any evidence of residents claiming to 'help' individual neighbours. One resident at GH1 stated that she '(went) to the shops' for the lady next door and all at GH2 stated that they 'helped' Mrs. Ho — the female residents ran errands, the male resident helped with the gardening.

Illustrations — By far the most predominant impression obtained of residents' attitudes to neighbours was one of an inclination not to be imposing towards them, to keep very much to themselves and to speak only when invited. Several comments indicated a desire on the part of residents to show them politeness but to act in a reserved way. Again there was the problem of obtaining precise answers to the direct questions asked.

Example (1)

Q   'What about the lady next door?
A   I know she lost her husband about a fortnight ago; I know that she told me herself.
Q   How often do you talk to her?
A   Well if she speaks back I don't ignore her if she's in back and I'm in back I have a word with her.
Q   When did you last talk to her?
A   'Cause we're good neighbours next door you know.
Q   When did you last talk to her?
A   Well I not seen her today.
Q   How long do you talk to her when you do see her?
A   Well I have a word with her well you can't do anything else. It's only manners, I been brought up like that.
Q   What do you talk to her about?
A   Well if she asks me if I'm alright I say yes.
Q   What else do you talk to her about?

77

A   If she asks me if I had a good day at work and things like that I
    say yes which I have today.
Q   Does she help you at all?
A   She would do if I were to ask her, yes.
Q   Do you help her?
A   I would do if she were to ask me, yes.
Q   What about the lady that side?
A   Oh them's alright next door.
Q   Do you like her that side?
A   Yes she's very nice, in fact both sides are good.
Q   How often do you see that lady?
A   Occasionally you know I've not seen them today though 'cause
    she's usually busy.
Q   When was the last time you saw her?
A   Well I generally see her at weekends.
Q   You saw her at the weekend?
A   Yes on Sunday when she's pegging her clothes out.
Q   When did you last talk to her, when was the last time you talked to
    her?
A   Last week when I spoke to her she says you alright and I said yes
    thank you, she always asks me if I've had a good day at work and
    I say yes which we have had a busy day today as well, been
    making little boxes to put drills in small ones and put them inside
    another and then putting them in boxes.
Q   What do you talk to her about?
A   Things in general.
Q   How long do you speak to her for?
A   Well it just depends how long she wants to stop and speak to me
    for.
Q   Does she help you?
A   She would if were to ask her, yes.
Q   Do you help her?
A   I would yes there's a job I'd like to do if I could have it I love to
    help old people. I looked after my grandma when I had her you
    know, she had very high blood pressure, she couldn't get down I
    had job to do for her get down on floor and thinks like that for
    her 'cause she couldn't you know'.

Example (2)

Q   'Which neighbours do you know?
A   I don't know any of them.
Q   You don't know any of them?
A   I don't go asking them 'cause it's not my business to go and ask
    them. If they talk to me I talk to them'.

Example (3)

Q 'Which neighbours do you know that live round here?

A Well I don't know them by name, I only know that one at 61. I only know them by sight, one at the bottom of the road, very bottom with glasses on.

Q What do you talk about?

A Just pass the time of day. I don't tell her anything just say hello and that, I'm not one for neighbouring you know going and talking to them'.

(c) *Contact with friends:* When asked which friends they had, in the main residents stated co-residents and/or people 'at work'. Sometimes the latter were referred to 'en bloc', other times individuals were named. The majority of other friends mentioned were people from the residents' previous places of residence. Three residents said 'no one', 'no one special' or 'no one in particular' (outside mentioning co-residents). Apart from the occasional exception, each resident named no more than two 'friends' (excluding co-residents/workmates). 'Friends' mentioned were mostly people they had known over a long period of time although there were a few cases of friendships made during the time they had been in the group home, for example, residents from GH3 mentioned a local police-man 'friend' who visited them; Beryl at GH2 mentioned individual 'friends' at a local youth club she had joined. Several of the 'friends' mentioned had ordinary employment and this is particularly striking in relation to those group home residents who did *not* have ordinary jobs — of 18 residents without ordinary jobs, 13 claimed to have one or more 'friends' with an ordinary job.

Residents were asked how often they 'saw their 'friends'. Co-residents being excluded, as would be expected, workmates were seen daily (excluding weekends) though no one admitted to 'seeing' workmates out-side work. Those 'friends' from residents' previous places of residence were generally only 'seen' when one of the group home members visited the unit concerned. These visits were usually only occasional — 'monthly', 'every three months' or less. Other types of 'friend' contact were varied; very few were daily or weekly, these being (GH1) Sylvia-Albert (daily); Doris/Barbara A.-Mr. and Mrs. Wheatley, Betty and Bill (voluntary visitors) (weekly); (GH2) Bertha-Mabel (weekly); (GH4) Doreen-John (daily), Hilary (few times a week); (GH5) Audrey-Mrs. G. (weekly); (GH6) Henry-mates in local pub (weekly).

Illustrations — Residents described continued friendships with people whom they had left behind in the hospital or hostel, or with those whom they had known years before in a hospital but who had since been 'moved on' elsewhere. In contrast there were those who shunned 'the hospital' and anyone associated with it on the grounds that they were now living

79

more independently and did not wish to be reminded of their past circumstances.

Example (1)

Q 'What friends have you got?

A I got them here. I don't bother with anyone else. I'm not going back to that place'.

Example (2)

Q 'What other friends have you got?

A No more.

Q Are you sure?

A Yes, I talk to Gladys an' all them oh I got one or two outside but not in here I don't bother with them outside. There's plenty of people but they not your friends'.

Example (3)

Q 'How often do you go to see him (in hospital)?

A He's had a chance you know to come here and if he'd have come here he'd have had a right time with us you know gone out and shown him round Sheffield with him he's very bad feet though you know he's bad at walking.

Q How often do you go to (the hospital)?

A Every month about.

Q Every time you go you speak to him do you?

A Yes every time.

Q How long do you talk to him for?

A Oh a long time if he's going on holidays he always asks if I'm going with him you know for company you know to walk with him to show him round shops.

Q Good idea. What do you talk to him about when you see him?

A I says to him I don't know why Pop you're getting on you know with age as I am I says I don't know why you shouldn't have took this chance to have house I says there's nothing to do just general what have you, go out and have a walk if there's any things they want you to do Bertha and Gladys will do it I says you always make your own bed. He says I don't think it would be any good to me I says it would you know what your dad told you when he come to see you he says what he says you were a bloomin' fool to yourself you should have took it 'cause it would have been nearer for your dad to come and see you 'cause your dad live near here you know he says I know but I don't like leaving kitchens I says look somebody's got to have another chance let the young ones go at it I says they're younger than you Ellis and all that lot Bill Savage and all that lot I says let them have a go I says we're getting on now and we can't stand it no longer somebody's got to go'.

(d) *Contact with official support networks:* Residents stated the support workers with whom they came into contact and the sorts of help they received from them. They were asked also to rate their liking of each support workers on the same 5-point scale. As a comment, it is important to take account of the extent of feeling expressed by residents to support workers as such attitudes influence the nature and quality of relationships and the effectiveness of support given. On the grounds that support workers were in an official 'helping' role, it might be supposed that they would have been thought of favourably. By and large, this was in fact the case as there were few answers other than 'strongly like' or 'quite like'; 'indifferent' was given in a very small number of cases, for example, 'she's alright, I suppose', 'I don't mind her', usually in referring to support workers who only visited the home on an occasional basis; 4 residents said they 'quite dislike(d)' a support worker — 3 from GH2 expressed this view towards one of the Home Helps.

Findings from the participant-observation part of this study supported this evidence as on the whole there were very few incidents where residents were heard to complain about or criticise official support workers. Most comments made of support workers in their absence were of a very favourable kind, indicating the extent of positive feeling residents bore towards them. When together, added confirmation was provided of the extent of such feelings, for it was seen that residents addressed support workers in ways that could be described as respectful, friendly or trusting. Whereas individual residents may have harboured some possible more negative feelings towards one or more support workers these were not clearly apparent, hence when occasional critical comments were made openly they were easily noticed.

In one home, GH2, the residents complained that the Home Help was not buying enough food for them and that often she bought them food they disliked. It was not clear whether they confronted her with this; most probably they preferred to complain 'behind her back'. The Social Work Assistant endorsed the fact that the Home Help was inclined to purchase items without the residents' approval. 'She takes one or more of them on Fridays to the supermarket when she does her main shopping but just throws articles in the trolley without considering whoever accompanies her. They're just used as packhorses when it comes down to it'. On several occasions one or more residents criticised at Home Help for interferring, though these one-sided comments were sometimes mediated with warmer sentiments shows towards her. In GH3, resentment reigned against the Nursing Officer whom, it was alleged, had sold them a television set — 'he took ten pounds from each of us' — which had broken down soon afterwards. Residents expressed the view that he had made several visits to the home in the early days, had managed to secure various articles of furniture for them and, in the process, had sold them a television set of his own, since when he had stopped visiting. This was a particularly unusual situation in that it placed a support worker in a position where residents were no longer prepared to place trust in him and hence could well have had more serious consequences.

Returning to the interviews with residents, most of the known official support workers were mentioned as being 'seen' by one or more of them. Residents referred to those who visited them, for example, Social Workers, Social Work Assistants, Home Helps and others, who 'helped' them (but did not necessarily visit the home). Some residents, despite their living in the same home as one another, mentioned different 'visitors' although such 'visitors' came to see all members of a group. Six residents claimed to have received 'help' from an ATC staff-member and 12 mentioned one or more staff-members from their previous place of residence.

The following table contains a categorisation of the types of help residents claimed to have received from individual support workers. For illustrative purposes, examples of their own words are included:

Type of help placed in order of frequency of it being mentioned	*Overall number of times mentioned by residents in respect of individual support workers*
Personal care:	
Care, advice, information, dealing with problems — 'she looks after us', 'he's interested in us', 'see if we're alright', 'just stops (by) a bit', 'helps you — you know what I mean', 'just talks to use', 'gives me confidence'.	28*
Finance:	
'sorts out money', 'pays rent', 'sorts out our spends'.	27
Housework:	
Variety of home-based chores — 'dusts chairs, walls', 'cleans floors', 'washes pots', 'cleans windows', 'helps with decorations', 'cuts down curtains', 'helps with washer', 'makes dinners', 'tidies up'.	22

* More may have stated this than has been acknowledged, such comments being additional to the main points made.

Type of help placed in order of frequency of it being mentioned	Overall number of times mentioned by residents in respect of individual support workers
Shopping:	
'helps me with shopping', 'fetches few things'.	15
Teaching:	
'teaches us to shop, cook', 'teaches me swimming', 'teaches me to play dominoes', 'teaches me how to use money', 'teaches me the job, to read and write, embroidery'.	15
Clothing:	
'sorts out clothes', 'gets me clothes'.	8
Presents and gifts	7
'mends things', 'takes things up', 'shortens trousers'.	7
arranges/provides transport to hospital/GP appointments	6
'does our hair'	5
'fixes holidays, trips'	3
'go out together'	3
'writes my letters'	3
'deals with tablets'	2
'gets our food cheap'	2
'gives us messages'	2
'car lifts'	1
'fixes vacuum, plugs'	1
'gets me silks'	1

As a comment on the above table, it is perhaps surprising, given that many staff later stated (Section B, ix) that they were trying to encourage the independence of group home residents, that 'teaching' tasks were placed relatively low down in the list. The personal care function was most frequently mentioned: this covered a wide range of general tasks including the giving of practical advice, support and information; showing concern, interest and consideration for the welfare of individual residents; or being someone with whom they could talk, confide in and discuss their personal problems. Assistance with finances was the other main form of help acknowledged, perhaps indicating the relatively low ability of the groups overall to manage their finances without support (only GH3 handled its finances independently). The majority of references to 'teaching' help were concerned with 'cooking' either on the part of the Home Helps or an outside volunteer as in the case of GH1 and 4. The other 'help' mentioned covers a very wide variety of tasks and is an indication of the type of support residents needed. Jobs such as mending and shortening garments were often done in the support workers' 'own time'.

Illustrations — Residents were very clear about whether or not they liked individual support workers. Those they liked, they mostly liked very much; liking was expressed at a personal level and no distinctions could be drawn between liking for different types of worker. As a comment, it is important that residents are given support from people whom they trust and can feel friendly towards.

Example (1) Loyalty was expressed in one resident's feelings towards a person:

> 'I tell you why I don't like her 'cause she bosses (Social Work Assistant) about and I like her'.

Example (2)

Q 'What about X how do you feel about her?
A She's alright no but you know she keeps saying what you done with your money so I says oh I just you know I told her and then she says you should have two or three pounds put away now so I says what with buying these look and I took a cake out of my bag and showed her oh I know she says but you shouldn't do you know......'

Example (3)

Q 'What help do you get from X?
A Oh she asks me questions like if I want anything she wanted to see if I wanted her to get a chair I said I don't want a chair it's a wardrobe I want she was going to go with me for it but I thought well I could get it myself I'm big enough to get it myself'.

(e) *Benefactor*

Edgerton (1967) first coined this term to denote those who help mentally handicapped people with their problems, including assisting with the practical difficulties of coping with everyday matters and the multifold problem of 'passing' (being accepted socially as normal) and 'denying' (that they are mentally handicapped). His study of the experiences of ex-hospitalised people living in the community concludes that 'in general, the ex-patient succeeds in his efforts to sustain a life in the community only as well as he succeeds in locating and holding a benefactor' (p.204). Group home residents were asked whom was the first person that they turned to when they were in need of help. Answers given consisted of official support workers, co-residents and other outsiders (friend/relative) in a ratio $16\frac{1}{2}$*:4:$3\frac{1}{2}$*. Hence, it could be said that, over

---

* $\frac{1}{2}$ denotes an instance where a resident gives an either/or answer.

two-thirds of the total group of 24 residents acknowledge one of the official support workers as their 'benefactor'. The role of specific support workers needs to be stressed, for example, all at GH5 gave the Social Work Assistant and 3 at GH2 gave the Home Help/neighbour. As for those who 'turned to' co-residents, 2 were from GH4 who reciprocated a need for each other — 'I treat Doreen as though she were my own mother she meant a lot to me, you know, it upset me when I lost her' — another was John Rylands who mentioned his wife and the other was Beattie at GH3 who mentioned Gladys, her 'mother figure'. Three of those who claimed that they would 'turn to' an outside friend or relative came from the same home (GH1).

(f) *Leisure activities:*   Individual residents were asked how they spent their 'free time'. A wide range of activities was given and this follows in order of their popularity.

Type of leisure activity	Number of residents
Watching TV	17
Going to town, shops	6
Going to pub	5
Playing records	5
Gardening	4
Going to Gateway Club	4
Going for a walk	4
Listening to radio	4
Going dancing	3
Knitting	3
Rug-making	2
Sewing	2
Writing	2
Crayoning	1
Going to cinema	1
Seeing friends	1
Silks	1
Sorting out belongings	1
Swimming	1

Watching television was by far the most popular activity but was no more popular in one home than another; using local facilities (shops, going for walks, pub and cinema visits) accounted for a lot of their leisure time. Comparing the activities of those residents who were 'at home' with those 'employed' one particular difference emerged, being that the rather time-consuming handicraft activities such as knitting, sewing and rug-making were done, with only one exception, by residents based 'at home' during the day-time. However, when the activities of those residents in ordinary employment were compared with those of the rest, no real differences emerged, except, for example, that none in ordinary employment said they attended the Gateway Club.*

* The National Federation of Gateway Clubs was established by the National Society for Mentally Handicapped Children in 1966. Today there are between 400 and 500 Gateway Clubs throughout the UK, providing leisure activities for mentally handicapped children and adults.

(iii)   Summary: The above findings illustrate the nature and extent of contacts of individual residents with relatives, neighbours, friends and representatives of official support agencies. There was a general variation both between homes and between individuals residing in them.

Firstly, in relation to contact with relatives — 5 residents had no contacts (of whatever means); others averaged 2.3 contacts each, brothers/sisters being the most common; contacts were usually made by visits to the relative's home, though in a few instances it was recognised that a relative would visit the group home; almost half of the contacts were frequent, i.e. daily or weekly with GH1, 2 and 3 residents having proportionately more of these than the rest; most residents stated that they did not receive 'help' as such from relatives, although several claimed that relatives would help if asked or were in a position to do so; occasionally residents claimed that they 'helped' relatives in the form of doing housework or errands; several voiced strong attitudes towards individual relatives either of liking or resentment.

Secondly, contact with neighbours — all but three residents knew one or more neighbours; the majority knew a next door neighbour, and, additionally, approximately one half knew one or more living in the same road; residents from the same home did not always know the same neighbours; frequent contact was only made with a few neighbours and these were usually people living next door; the majority of contacts were short encounters — 'hello, how are you?' and suchlike; 11 neighbours overall were said to provide 'help' to individual residents from the six homes but this was mostly in the form of giving occasional advice and information and rarely practical aid; in general residents were reserved in their social contacts, only speaking to neighbours when they were spoken to.

Thirdly, contact with friends — in the main, residents stated as their friends co-residents and/or workmates; other friends were usually people from their previous places of residence; three residents said they had 'no one'; apart from the occasional exception, each resident stated that he/she had no more than two friends (excluding co-residents/workmates); there were very few examples of residents having friends in the community that they had made since moving to the homes; many residents not in open employment had friends in open employment; no residents in open employment saw their workmates outside work; friends from residents' previous homes were usually only seen when residents visited — such visits occured usually no more frequently than every month; there was evidence of residents not wanting friends from their previous homes.

Fourthly, contacts with official support workers — most residents stated that they liked individual support workers but there were also examples of their not liking or feeling indifferent towards them; in addition to those visiting the homes, help was acknowledged as being given by ATC staff and staff from residents' previous homes; the principal kind of help given was in the form of advice, emotional support and information, with help in financial matters running close second in rank order; help in the form of teaching was placed relatively low down; some residents criticised support workers both on a personnal level and in terms of their professional competence.

Lastly, concerning residents' 'benefactors' and leisure activities — over two thirds of residents said that they would turn to one of the official support workers if they needed help, others chose a co-resident, friend or relative; as to leisure activities, watching television was singled out the most popular, followed by the use of a range of community facilites, for example, shops, local pubs, cinema; handicraft activities such as rug-making, sewing, knitting, were with one exception only undertaken by those not 'at work' *i.e.* not at ATC or in open employment; there were no differences observed in the activities of residents in open employment from those of other residents, apart from the fact that the former did not claim to attend the Gateway Club.

To what extent can care be provided by the community? The above evidence illustrates how group home residents depend mainly on the support provided through official networks. There was little data pointing to the fact that contacts with and support from relatives, neighbours and friends can be established merely by placing mentally handicapped people to live in the community. They need help and encouragement in initiating such contacts which is perhaps not surprising given that they have previously lived in rather different, more protective surroundings. The findings stress the need for official support workers to recognise the all-important role they can play in teaching residents to become independent, and in assisting their community integration by helping to foster their links with neighbours, workmates and relatives. Furthermore, there is a role for them as educators to inform members of a local public on issues relating to mental handicap, its meaning and the types of background experienced by those mentally handicapped people moving into the community from somewhere like a hostel or hospital. The value of using a neighbour as an official support worker was particularly acknowledged in the case of one home and this has wider uses for the general development of group home care.

There is something like a natural instinct on the part of most neighbours 'not to want to interfere' and despite the fact that some may wish to help, they may at the same time feel reluctant without the outside encouragement. Similarly, it should be recognised that mentally handicapped people living together in a group home may not need further help nor desire further social contacts. They may be satisfied with the company they already have — co-residents, people 'at work' and so on — and these feelings should be respected. Given, however, that some degree of outside suppport is provided it may be the long-term aim of official support workers to find means of transferring these responsibilities to willing individuals living in the community as a gradual move towards providing care by the community.

The nature and extent of neigbour contact may relate to the type of neighbourhood area wherein the home is situated. One can compare, for example, contacts made by residents from the GH1 home placed in a good, mainly owner-occupied residential area with those made by residents from the GH2 or 3 homes placed in poorer, mainly council propertied areas and present a case that geographical location is one factor in determining the amount and type of neighbourhood contacts made. Residents from GH2 and 3 claimed that they said 'hello' to several people living in the road whom they did not 'know' as such. Maybe this sort of natural informal greeting with neighbours is more commonplace in some areas or types of areas than in others. Individuals vary in their willingness to act sociably with apparant strangers but judging from the series of general statements suggesting a more likely inclination for residents to speak only when spoken to, it might be concluded that most neighbour contacts were not initiated by the group home residents.

Another point concerns the references made by some individual mentally handicapped people to the help they received from official support workers other than those that visited their home more or less routinely. In particular, some mentioned training centre staff and this is singularly important in view of the need to coordinate links between day and residential care staff. A wide range of both academic and social skills are needed for a person to survive with relative independence in the community and the activities and teaching conducted in training centres could be closely directed towards these specific ends. The findings might be interpreted as suggesting a need for more effective working partnerships among all representatives of official support agencies having contacts with residents from group homes.

Lastly, it is useful to relate these findings to those from some of the neighbourhood studies that have been conducted. On the basis of selected material, three points emerge as relevant: firstly, the studies showed that people tended to use informal support in preference to the formal type. People cope with problems through the use of informal social resources, or an 'interpersonal environment' composed of family and friends, neighbours and work colleagues, (Gurin et al. (1960); Mayer and Timms (1970)). The contrasting findings of the present study concerned with the mentally handicapped highlight the potential dangers of taking people out of their locality in the first place and hence their having to relay on official support. The emphasis made on the use of official support underlines the need for support workers to encourage informal contacts on the part of residents rather than expect these to grow naturally.

The other two points concern the type of neighbour contact received. The first is that studies of patterns of urban social interaction have tended to question the need for 'good neighbours' based on the conclusion that contacts within neighbours are, on the whole, limited. (See, for example, Dennis (1963)). Pahl (1970) showed that 'only those of similar social status are defined as neighbours' and argued that the higher the social status of the neigbourhood, the more neighbours are seen 'non-people'. Others such as Glass (1948), Mitchell et al. (1954) and Mann (1965) have suggested that physical proximity does not inevitably reduce social distance (and, in fact, might even increase it.).

The second point is that, where neighbour contact does exist, it is usually confined to people living in the same streeet. Willmott's (1962) study of Stevenage New Town showed, for example, that three-quarters of the visitors received by individuals came from 'a very small area about one-quarter to one-half the size of a neighbourhood'. In fact, most either lived next door or in the same street. Taking both these findings as comprising one norm for evaluating community intergration as experienced by the group home residents of the present study, it comes as no immediate surprise that their contacts were also limited: contact with a next door neighbour was the type that stood out usually as the most predominant, and even this could not be taken for granted. In several instances this type of contact was not evident and in others probably would not have been so without external intervention.

Overview

The findings from the above sections (1 to 4) can be brought together in order to illustrate a number of points. Firstly, it is possible to draw on data of the previous background of residents to illuminate the changes in some of the assessment scores. Most marked improvements occurred in the scores of GH2 residents, but according to background file information, four out of six of this group had spent at least ten years in hospital prior to being moved to a group home. All residents at GH3 had spent at least ten years in hospital prior to the group home and each of these residents had on average improved on nine out of the twenty-four domains measured on the assessment instrument (most commonly Independent Functioning, Economic Activity, Vocational Activity, Self-direction, Responsibility, anti-social Behaviour, Rebellious Behaviour, Untrustworthy Behaviour, Psychological Disturbances), the remaining domains showing a dominance of 'no change' in scores.

Other residents with a background of ten or more years hospitalisation had shown exceptional improvements in the assessment scores over the two year period — for example, the two residents from GH5 improved on thirteen and eight out of the twenty-four domains; the one resident at GH6 who had also been assessed as 'ineducable' during childhood improved on ten domains including sub-domains 'money handling', 'budgeting' and 'reading'. The two residents who had each spent in excess of twenty years in a penal unit for mentally disordered offenders (Ronnie, GH3; Maud, GH5) both made impressive gains on the assessment, improving on eleven and thirteen (out of twenty-four) domains respectively. Residents at GH4 had, as a group, deteriorated on the assessment, yet in contrast to those residents from other homes, none had previous hospital experience. Instead each member of this group had gone from the family home to live in a hostel and then on to the group home having spent the majority of their life living at home with a relative. Furthermore, GH4 was the most recently set up home, residents having only moved in two or three months prior to the initial assessment taking place. Thus, more than in the case of any other home, the two-year assessment illustrated changes in individuals during the settling-in stage.

Despite the disadvantages of living in an institution for a long period of time and the well-known effects that institutional life can have on an individual, for example, disorientation, loss of incentive, the data showed that previous long-term hospitalisation was not related to a low level of skill learning by individuals within the group homes. In fact, quite the opposite was shown, as strongest individual improvements were made mostly by residents who had experienced long-term hospitalisation, whilst the only group home showing an overall deterioration was that occupied by residents who had not spent any time in hospital. This finding contradicts common opinion that mentally handicapped people with the most favourable chances of community rehabilitation are those who have spent least time away from the community.

How do the findings from the participant observation study on the group behaviour of residents link up with those from the two-year assessment? Some interesting points emerge for discussion. For example, the data explained the nature and function of role-taking that had occurred for organising housework, particularly in the larger homes, GH1, 2 and 3. There had been 'across the board' gains in each of these homes in domains that wre group-skill orientated (headed Self-direction, Responsibility, Socialisation), being most marked in such sub-domains as persistence, general responsibility, consideration for others, awareness of and interaction with others. It has been argued, in Section 3, that role performance has raised the morale of individual residents and contributed significantly to the essential harmony of the home, for example, Bertha at GH3 whose job of 'cooking for the family' gave her pride and determination. It is thus not surprising that gains in these (group-skill) areas were made and served to underline the importance of such skills when a relatively large number of people (five) are placed together in an ordinary house.

The group behaviour study (Section 3) has shown how several concepts applicable in earlier studies of small group behaviour, for example, leaders and followers, scapegoats, were relevant to understanding the pattern of relationships within the group homes. The two obvious 'leaders', John

(GH2), Gladys (GH3) had made encouraging gains on the assessment. John, it will be remembered, was recognised as a leader of the 'maintenance function' type (encouraging, harmonising, compromising, gatekeeping), whereas Gladys' leadership stemmed mainly from her superior ability to carry out tasks (initiating, information seeking and giving, clarifying). John's gains were mainly on Part II of the A-B scale in the reduction of 'maladaptive behaviour' where he showed signs of improved behaviour in several areas. This is consistent with the overall picture for GH2 where many individual maladaptive behaviours were reduced or eliminated. Gladys showed improvement in approximately half of the domains with a fairly equal spread across Parts I and II, which is consistent with her role of 'all-round' leader — as a leader she always took the initiative, was always active and played her part in a wide range of domestic tasks.

The scapegoating of George Maybury (GH3) mainly on acccount of his idleness and lack of involvement with the group showed up to an extent in the score losses he made on Part I domains. He deteriorated on items such as miscellaneous independent functioning, budgeting, errands, conversation and general domestic activity. Sylvia Beck (GH1) had been 'blamed' for a number of reasons by members of the group but this showed up in the opposite way in her assessment scores. She had made more gains than any of her co-residents (in thirteen out of the twenty-four domains). By way of accounting for this, Section 3 referred to observed changes in Sylvia throughout the two-year assessment period — she had become more confident and able to undertake domestic tasks, members of the group showed her more tolerance, her 'outside' relationship with Albert improved. From being a vulnerable newcomer to the group home, she had achieved a stable compromise with the other residents. George, on the other hand, had consistently refused to become drawn in to any of the group's activities, whether of the work or leisure kind which accounted for the unrelenting criticisms made of him by other group members.

Is the effect of being 'mothered' likely to be associated with an individual improving or deteriorating in skill-learning and behaviour? 'Mothering' strikes connotations of doing everything for someone, encouraging their dependence rather than independence. If this is true then one might expect that on Part I domains, certainly, an individual's chances of improving would be inhibited by 'mothering'. On the other hand, the effect of 'mothering' may be that an individual experiences stability and security in a relationship which may be associated with personal development and overcoming feelings of unworthiness. The two examples of 'mothered' individuals discussed in Section 3 data, Beryl (GH2) and Beattie (GH3) improved on almost half, including five out of ten on Part I (Personal Independence). These two examples thus showed that 'mothering' was related to an increase in independence of the person being 'mothered'.

The main sub-group described in Section 3 was that consisting of Ruth and Shirley at GH4. It might be expected that a close friendship between two people would have positive consequences in terms of assessment, gains being made by one or both of them. This was not the case as both residents showed a pattern of either making no gains or deteriorating — Shirley had more losses than any other group home resident. Section 3 also referred to individual difficult behaviour manifested in group homes and this observation is shown up in the assessment scores — Barbara Turnship had more losses than any other resident in GH1, Doris Grantham at GH2 showed a loss on Rebellious Behaviour.

Have outside social contacts had any bearing on individual resident scores? The highest number of gains at GH1 were made firstly by Sylvia and then Brenda, both having in common the fact that they had 'steady' boyfriends with whom they spent a large part of their leisure time. GH2 showed the highest overall number of gains and had also the highest number of local neighbourhood contacts (four out of five residents stated they knew 'one or two' neighbours in addition to Mrs. H. — the Home Help/next door neighbour). All at GH2 said they 'strongly liked' Mrs H. and the value of having a neighbour who is also employed as a Home Help deserves to be stressed. Both homes with a permanent Home Help input (GH2 and 5) made comparatively strong gains on Domestic Activity, although it is worth mentioning that the resident at GH6 also gained here without Home Help support.

There were comparatively high improvements at GH2, 3 and 6 on the sub-domain Money-Handling — these might easily be accounted for in the last two cases as at GH3 residents became fully independent of outside support for budgeting and the payment of bills and at GH6 the Social Worker had concentrated on training Henry to understand money and budgeting. There had *not* been improvements at GH1 and 4 in the sub-domain Food Preperation, although this might have been expected given the regular input of Paddy, the visiting cookery teacher. It has already been stated that GH1 residents showed marked improvements on group skills (domains Self-Direction, Responsibility, Socialisation) and this may well be related to the group casework approach of the Social Work Assistant. GH5 residents referred to the help they received from people in the local shops and this is borne out in Audrey's scores (sub-domains Money Handling and Budgeting, Shopping Skills).

Other points stand out from the data, for example, GH1, 2 and 3 residents had proportionately more frequent (*i.e.* daily or weekly) contacts with relatives than other residents despite the high proportion from this group as a whole that had spent many years living in hospital. Findings from Sections 3iv.a. and 4ii.d. interrelate concerning the role of support workers as friends and advisers. The predominant type of 'help' acknowledged by residents in describing the role of support workers (see Table D ii.d.) was that of giving advice, information and help in solving personnal problems. Data from the other sections support this emphasising the fundamental contribution of this type of role for individual resident and group development. There had been countless incidents where minor and major problems had arisen for individual residents and, being limited in their ability to work towards a satisfactory solution, a trusting relationship with an outside figure had proved its value. This reliance on certain members of the official support network again was confirmed by findings from Section 4 ii.e. when two-thirds of group home residents admitted to turning to one of the official workers before any other such as a friend, relative or neighbour if they were ever in need of help.

CHAPTER 4

The Official Support System

This section is concerned with issues relating to the administration and basic operation of the group homes and presents the findings from two main sources, (a) an interview checklist administered to individual staff and (b) departmental file data.

As regards (a) the checklist covered ten items, giving a total of thirty-seven questions (Appendix C). The majority of the questions were 'fact-finders' in that their purpose was to discover basic facts concerning the homes, for example, 'What formal decision-making bodies exist for the group home?', 'How are decisions reached about.....' The remainder were 'opinion-finders' in that their purpose was to discover personal and/or professional opinions on relevant issues, for example 'What is your personal opinion as to whether.....?', 'For whom do you think group homes should be provided?' The overall purpose of devising this type of checklist had been to collect information on the administration, organisation and operation of the homes since their early stages of development. Hence it was necessary that the checklist should cover a wide range of items concerning the functioning of the homes and the role of the staff at different levels. In the main the questions included in this checklist were 'policy-oriented' in that they had been worded in such terms, that they assumed some degree of formal policy to have existed in relation to each of the respective items. A copy of the checklist had been given to a number of support workers for each of the homes up to and including the managerial level of Area Officer. The exception had been GH3 where other non-Social Services Department officers had been included, owing to the peculiar nature of that particular scheme.

Figure A indicates the organisational structure of fieldwork teams within the Social Services Department. Group home provision was at the basic level administered through the Area teams and hence for the present purpose only the outline structure of a typical Area team is given. The lines drawn between positions represent an official hierarchy of authority from the Departmental Director downwards. However, the actual nature of relationships among workers for each group home situation varied according to individual circumstance, and hence Figure A must be taken as a model rather than a true representation of the management structure for any given case. Furthermore, whereas Home

Help Services were organised on an Area Basis (and hence managerially accountable to the respective Area Officer) the position they occupy in Figure A should not be taken to indicate the status of their members in relation to Social Workers in the Area Team.

Table 3 gives the numbers and types of support staff who responded to the questions of the checklist. It includes all but two staff members who, during the time of the present study had been officially involved in providing support to the homes and additional others, such as Home Helps, who had been involved prior to the study. Hence the checklist was administered to the whole range of staff members within each Area Team for each respective group home. By studying the answers given by the members of each support team to each separate question, conclusions could be drawn on each separate checklist item. This 'cross-checking' method proved a basis for understanding both the extent of knowledge among staff members and how particular organisational processes and procedures were perceived at different levels within the hierarchy.

Figure A

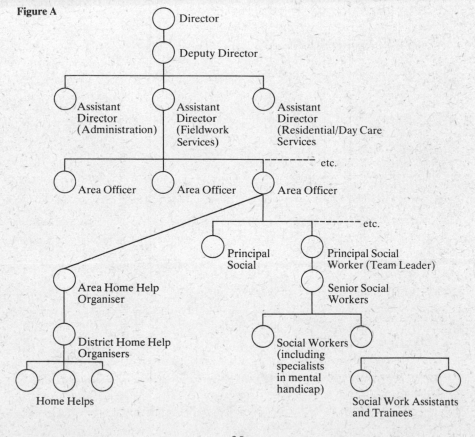

Table 3   Type of staff member completing checklist for each group home

Name of Home	TYPE OF STAFF MEMBER											Total per Home
	Area Officer	Principal Social Worker	Social Worker	Welfare Assistant	Area Home Help Organiser	District Home Help Organiser	Home Help 1	Home Help 2	Nursing Officer	Ward Sister	Nursing Assistant	
GH1	/*	/*	/	/	/*	/*	/*	/				7
GH2	/	/	/	/	/	/	/	/				8
GH3	/	/	/	/								5
GH4	/*	/*	/	/	/*	/*	/*	/	/	/	/	7
GH5	/	/	/	/	/	/	/	/				7
GH6	/	/	/	/	/	/	/	/				7
Overall Total of Respondents**												41

* Staff member is (was) responsible for both GH1 and 4

** Overall total of actual staff members filling in a checklist = 36
(accounting for those from GH1 and 4 who 'doubled-up')

Checklists were completed by the research worker for each staff member in turn — questions being asked in a face-to-face interview situation, though no attempt was made to deal with specific staff members or homes in a particular order. Questions were posed both in the order and format in which they were presented on the checklist though occasional clarifications of meaning were given. Answers were written in although some rewording took place to elucidate or summarise. In the case of respondents giving their opinions on subjects, answers were not easily comparable with one another, whereas in the case of those answers of a more factual kind, this problem did not strictly arise. One problem in any interview-type situation concerns the reliability of the answers. This was not tested using standard interrater reliability techniques, but then the checklist in the main sought to elicit facts on specific issues rather than opinions, and the giving of this type of information is much less, if at all, subject to influence by the person administering the checklist. Furthermore, the checklist covered much observable fact thus there would have been little point in deception or exaggeration. Each respondent was told that his colleagues within the respective support team and similarly-placed staff members in other support teams were being asked the checklist questions, hence it was thought even less likely that facts would be changed deliberately or exaggerated by individuals. On the other hand, it could be argued that this may have contributed to a desire on behalf of particular individuals to present answers that were consistent with those of specific colleagues. Finally, all respondents were informed that the checklist data would be handled confidentially and thus not be available to other members of the respective support team or to any officers inside or outside the Department, but instead a report based on their findings would be eventually available to all respondents for comment.

With regard to (b) the Social Services Department kept a file on each group home containing documents relating, in particular, to how each home started off. In overall terms they dealt with policy and administrative arrangements and gave the views of certain individuals on matters such as client selection, staffing support, administrative accountability and the status of the residents in question. They often also included a record of home visits. These files differed in detail, in some cases providing the basis for an elaborate account of how an issue was managed and in others, only fragments of information were available throwing very little light on how matters became eventually resolved.

SECTION 1 — **Early Policy Arrangements**

(i) *Joint action by Health and Social Service Departments*

The file with by far the most information was that of GH5 which provided a full description of how the home was set up in terms of the relative responsibilities of both the agencies concerned.

The earliest reference consisted of an approach made by a representative from the then Trent Regional Health Board (RHB) to the Director of Social Services in Sheffield suggesting 'a cooperative enterprise between the hospital and the Social Services Department'. It introduced the fact that a residential facility situated within the grounds of a district general hospital could be made available for the purposes of rehabilitating a group of mentally handicapped people selected from one of the wards. It proposed that '(they) would of course have to be discharged into the care of the Local Authority.....' and provided estimates of the various capital and revenue costs that would be involved.

'..... we have approximately 100 female mentally handicapped patients in K. Ward at the (hospital). All the patients were assessed some time ago and it is known that thirteen are high grade and suitable for discharge. I understand from the hospital that it is unlikely that you will be able to find places for them in the near future. A scheme has been suggested which, by a cooperative enterprise between the hospital and the Social Services Department, the Local Authority would be able to undertake the care of some of the patients.... the (facility) is used as residential accommodation for undergraduate medical students. Alternative accommodation has recently been provided for the medical students and (this facility) is now available for other use. It has been suggested that with the minimum expenditure (this facility) could be used as hostel accommodation for five mentally handicapped patients from K. Ward. The patients currently work in the hospital although it is hoped that work might be found for them outside the hospital. They would of course have to be discharged into the care of the Local Authority.....'

A more formal offer was later made to the Director of Social Services to take over the residential facility and this enclosed the following points of information:

'.....1. The capital cost of £3,100 will be met by the Regional Hospital Board.

2. The Board will have to charge a rental but it has been agreed that this charge would be nominal only.

3. It will be necessary to charge for services, e.g. light, heat, water, etc. You may feel that an agreed overall charge for these services would be less cumbersome than having to meter the consumption.

4. The Hospital Authorities will be responsible for repairs, but the Corporation responsible for any redecorations that may be necessary.

5. In Dr. L's letter of 12.1.73 he suggested that if the (facility) was used as a hostel it should be available only until new units to be built under the Sheffield Project (SDP) were operational. It is now felt that the (facility) could be made available as a hostel for a much longer period — say seven years.

6. I can confirm that including additional fire safety measures which will be carried out in the capital work mentioned in pt. 1, the Fire Authorities are satisfied on the fire precautions in the building.....

Three months later, the Director wrote back to the RHB stating that the recommendation of the Social Services Committee to take up this offer had been 'approved by the City Council'. This letter prompted a reply from the District Administrator that agreed to 'take necessary steps to see that the alterations that (were) necessary.....(would be) carried out as quickly as possible'.

The procedure was cut and dried but for confusion over other administrative arrangements. The minutes of an Inter-Disciplinary Working Party meeting stated that, '..... Dr. — (Medical Consultant) did not wish the Local Authority to run the hostel and ..... that a meeting had been arranged when it was hoped that a solution would be reached.....' The Medical Consultant preferred that the group home should be set up and administered by the original Working Party (consisting of Health Service personnel). However, the offer had been made and been accepted by the Social Services Department at least simultaneous with if not before these sentiments were expressed by the Consultant, such that soon afterwards the minutes of a Working Party meeting stated, 'a simple written agreement between the RHB and the Sheffield Corporation was being prepared by representatives of both authorities. It was noted that the selection of patients could still be made by (the two Medical Consultants) and that Mrs. A. (Senior Occupational Therapist based at the hospital) would be involved in the O.T. service in the unit'. Some time later it was reported that conversions had been completed and negotiations would be needed between the Health and Social Services Departments 'in order to bring the unit into use'. The unit had been cleaned by patients of the hospital's O.T. department and it was intended 'that (it) would be used during the day until the first group of patients were ready to move into the accommodation.....'. It was also made clear that 'after the first group had completed their stay the unit would be used for Local Authority patients'.

In the file of GH3 a Principal Social Worker's report described the initial action prompting the acquisition of the group home. 'A number of hospital residents' had been referred to Social Services as being in request of Part III accommodation (National Assistance Act, 1948), yet 'From interviews with these residents it became clear that a number of them would probably not require the more sheltered environment of Part III accommodation and that they wanted to live in more independent accommodation. Other factors considered were the lengthy waiting lists for Part III accommodation and a desire to ensure that residents who had known one another for many years had the opportunity to stay together'. The writer went on to say that

'it was therefore decided to use the Domestic Unit at (OH2) which was a three-bedroomed detached house to assess the residents concerned and provide any preparation required. Nursing staff at (OH2) assumed responsibility for selecting the residents to form the Group. Later on from discussion with the

99

residents and the Domestic Unit, Group Nurse 1 gained the impression that their progress as a Group was reasonably good at this stage. In general terms the members of the Group have between them sufficient skills to manage satisfactorily in a Group Home . . . . . '. The responsibility of the Social Services Department regarding certain items was mentioned,

' . . . . (the Principal Assistant, Mental Health) is liasing with the Housing Department for suitable accommodation in the Beighton/Woodhouse area. The house will be transferred to the Social Services Department and rented to the Group. I am not sure what the rent will be at this stage, or what the exact status of the residents will be, (I feel that they should be rent book holding tenants) . . . . . '. As to the arrangements for aftercare support, 'the suggestion is that both (OH2) Hospital and Social Services will be involved . . . . . I have suggested to (the Medical Consultant) that a named nurse be responsible for (OH2's) maintenance of contact with the Group Home residents'.

Both these accounts gave an indication of the kinds of negotiations that had taken place in the early days. They show initiatives employed by both agencies for tackling a problem requiring an innovatory approach and provide evidence of the different agency perceptions of client need. Perhaps their most important contribution was that they showed signs of the agencies' willingness to experiment with new forms of residential care, hence the evidence of unresolved difficulties was not unexpected.

(ii) *Administrative decisions*

The files showed in the case of GH4, 5 and 6 how the Director of Social Services intervened to negotiate with the DHSS on the question of the status of group home residents in terms of their financial entitlements. An extract from one of these files quoted the Director as saying 'though this is a group home, it is not classified as Part III accommodation within the meaning of the National Assistance Act as it is the Department's policy to encourage the residents to learn to live together as a reasonably independent community. The Department is responsible for furnishing the house and residents will be charged on a board and lodgings basis of £11 per week inclusive of food'. The purpose was to ensure that benefits were left unchanged, for in administrative terms, these were calculated on the basis of whether the home was 'to be classed as Part III accommodation or a Family Group Home'.

The Assessments Section of the Department was informed of the formal arrangements made, and in the case of GH5, a memo was sent from the Area Officer to the Assessments Officer endorsing the view of the Director in order to ensure that the Assessments Officer had sufficient backing for making the special claim for financial entitlement: 'the objectives of (GH5) are to promote the capacity to lead an independent and free life within the community with help and support provided by Home Helps, Social Workers and appropriate psychiatric support. It should be the objective to give maximum financial independence to the residents at (GH5) to enable them to buy their own food and clothes, within charges agreed between the Local Authority and the Supplementary Benefits Commission'.

This view of encouraging the financial independence of residents was reinforced through the file documents relating to GH1, where, from the outset, the Area Officer took a stand in protesting over the initially agreed overall maintenance charge laid on residents as being 'totally out of proportion to today's cost of living'. The Department had intended to charge each resident a modest sum per week 'that would cover accommodation payments, food, domestic replacements, electricity, etc.' The Area Officer wrote in reply, '.....I do not wish to seem punitive but if they are to live an independent life in the community at some future date then I think we have a responsibility to start at this stage giving them a true indication of what money will buy and what one can do with a weekly wage'. The argument was eventually resolved in the Area Officer's favour.

The other main question dealt with in the files concerned staffing support and centred on the confusion experienced by at least two Area Officers in determining how this was to be arranged. For GH6 there were letters written by the Area Officer to the Deputy Director and the Principal Assistant (Mental Health):

'.....I would be most grateful if you could inform me whether you would see such help as was required being additional to our Area "quota" or whether such help should have to be made available out of our "quota".....'
'.....if schemes are to operate Divisionally (at Area level) with staff support provided out of the home help service I would have thought it important to think of a basically similar approach. If there are wide variations in conditions of service I would suggest the Department is heading for a lot of trouble, with staff grievances, etc. The group home represents an innovation as far as Sheffield is concerned and I would have thought it important enough to warrant careful, considered and clear thinking, with close evaluation and monitoring.....'

There were no replies in the file to the points raised and it appeared that the Area Officer had been left to decide on how best to provide support to the group home within existing available resources. He set out his ideas on the project though these were not taken up, and GH6 began with Home Help support taken from the Area 'quota' under usual terms and conditions.

'.....In total ignorance of other similar projects and Departmental thinking in relation to such projects, I would like to recommend the following establishment for (GH6):
Two part-time home helps operating on a four day on, four day off alternate system, the hours being 8 a.m. to 10 a.m. and 5 p.m. to 10 p.m. Monday to

Friday, and 9 a.m. to 12 noon, and 5 p.m. to 10 p.m. at weekends. This represents 51 hours per week, some 11 hours more than target. I would suggest a special recruitment to two such posts, the establishment not to come out of the Area quota for home helps. I would point out that Mrs. P. (Principal Assistant (Domiciliary Services)) has suggested an enhanced hourly rate for such workers, that a national agreement is in force for additional hourly rates for split duties and unusual hours and enhanced payments are made for weekend work, so that such a scheme would cost more than the normal fifty-one home help hours. These hours would be on a basis of five or six mentally handicapped occupants and might represent more than is required for an established community, but initially would be vital. The hope and expectation would be to avoid the (GH2) situation of the 'home helps' being disturbed and interrupted in off-duty periods and deterring their own hours of work. Essentially one is looking for people to work bad hours (split duties) and unusual hours (evenings and weekends) and I would maintain that such people will only be forthcoming if the job is made attractive with enhanced pay and good, fair working conditions which do not impose intolerable pressure and strain . . . . .'.

At GH1 the Area Officer had written of how Home Helps were to be 'specially chosen and prepared for the task of settling the girls in' and how she hoped that a proper assessment could take place later (in say three of four months) to ascertain what further support residents would require. Letters were written to senior administrative staff expressing concern over the lack of official policy in this regard, and the Area Officer proceeded in giving her own views on the potential of the project:

'. . . . . the hostel (not far from the group home) is in an area where it is likely to be relatively easy to find volunteers who are interested in such a project should this be necessary or desirable. The hostel is very interested and will be helping in the settling in process and the girls are to be encouraged to join in the social activities there.'
'. . . . . the ultimate aim will be to get those who are capable of independent living rehoused by the Housing Department but this will take a fairly lengthy period of observation and assessment before an approach can be made.'

(iii) *Summary*

The data illustrated the nature of innovations in policy on the part of the agencies concerned. The beginnings of the group homes had required specific initiatives to be taken and certain questions resolved before they could operate successfully. The files had shown good evidence of a lack of official Departmental policy towards some issues and a resultant confusion of middle management officers (AOs) in tackling their own schemes. This had eventually led to some 'common ground' being found, for example, in determining the financial entitlements of residents, but in other instances, for example, staffing support, with the absence of any overall policy initiative, Areas had been left to resolve their problems in their own contrived way. A constructive innovatory 'joint action' approach had been evident in the setting-up of two homes; in both cases the Area Health Authority (AHA) had approached the Local Authority on the matter of rehabilitating chosen residents and a working compromise between the two separate bodies had emerged. In one of these cases, the Local Authority representatives had shown an initiative that was both positive and innovatory in the context of inter-agency collaboration involving firstly a formal assessment of client needs and subsequent liaison with the Housing Department, AHA and DHSS to get the home set up. The question of ascertaining residents' entitlement to welfare benefit had in each case involved the intervention of the Departmental Director along with the necessity for several formal statements summing up the objective of each home as a means of authorising residents being classified as financially independent. There had been disagreement within the Department on this issue, with higher management (Assistant Director level) initially pushing for greater control over residents' finances and middle management (AO level) opting for more 'realistic' allowances and payments for basic services such as rent and fuel.

SECTION 2 — Selection, Preparation and Training of Residents

The procedures for the selection of group home residents, and the provision of preparation and training activities differed in relation to each of the six homes, although there were examples of some common factors. Knowledge and a general awareness of the relevant facts differed among the support workers serving each home — in broad terms these differences occurred between Social Work and Home Help staff and between direct care staff and managers. Only in the case of two homes, GH3 and 4, were there clearly distinguishable arrangements for preparing residents to live in the group home. There was evidence suggesting that some efforts were made in other homes to prepare residents but these were on a very minor scale and involved only selected residents. As for the provision of training and support following the move to the home, a varied pattern of arrangements was set up involving Social Work and Home Help staff. Home Helps were concerned with basic housework, shopping and some personal effects, for example, residents' clothing but involvement differed in relation to the group home, the personality of the Home Help and the length of time that the home had been established. A further difference concerned the extent to which a Home Help was involved in teaching residents as opposed to simply carrying out these tasks herself.

There were clear instructions that individual support workers lacked a defined role and this often had serious implications for the provision of support and the carrying out of tasks at the home level. In the selection of initial groups of residents, the relatively high involvement of the two Medical Consultants was common throughout, although the data provided no precise information of the basis on which most of these decisions were made. There was evidence of the use of an exchange system where residents were selected from a hospital that was able to make available a bed for a person whom it had been decided should no longer remain in the group home. However, there were examples of more careful selection procedures, such as those operating for GH3 and 4, where relatively large groups of candidates were initially chosen from which two smaller groups were selected following a period of assessment. In the case of at least two homes, the attached Social Worker formally advertised the need to find suitable home candidates by liaison with Social Work staff from other Area offices.

In relation to changes that occurred in the selection procedures, evidence from three homes indicated that the current policy was for residents to be chosen by Social Work staff directly involved in the homes and through relatively formal means, consisting of sending written notification and details of a vacancy to several managerial and fieldwork officers within the Department inviting them to make a recommendation. Reports on suitable candidates would be prepared and relevant discussions would follow. The current position in other homes was unclear, concluding that a future selection policy had yet to be decided. On the methods of introducing residents to homes, there was more conformity. For example, in relation to the original groupings, introduction consisted of making one or more prior visits to the home for the purpose of enabling residents to take a general look around. At GH6 additional acitivities were arranged in order to introduce residents to one another as they each came from different places. As for the admission of a subsequent resident to the group, introduction consisted of inviting the person for a meal, followed by separate discussions conducted by the Social Worker with the parties involved, followed by a weekend or overnight stay and ending with a trial stay period.

GH3 residents received training prior to their move in a special 'domestic training unit' within the grounds of the hospital where they resided. This training period lasted for approximately eighteen months and covered 'basic housekeeping, domestic science, cookery, use of slot meters for fuel payments, shopping for small and large items'. For the first part of this period 'a nurse was with them at all times' and for the remainder they were aided by a Nursing Assistant 'under supervision'. According to the Nursing Assistant interviewed, training was only provided to the female members of the group, hence it was not clear what, if anything, was provided for the two males in the way of preparation and training for group home living. In the case of GH4, residents were taught some cookery and other domestic skills in weekly evening sessions held by Social Work staff with the aid of volunteers. These sessions took place prior to the residents being moved out; they were held in a separate house belonging to the Department and attended by a number of LA hostel residents.

(i) Recommendations for group home living

Some of the files contained short reports or statements made by a Social Worker or Medical Consultant that described individual clients prior to their move to a group home. These usually included either an explicit or an implicit recommendation for group home or more independent living for a client and in so doing discussed the client's social competence and personality.

'She was very slow in developing, both physically and mentally but has always been a pleasant personality, gradually developing her skills in talking, reading, writing and domestic tasks. She can now manage all her own needs, and is now capable of life in the community with a minor degree of supervision.'

In particular, self-care and household tasks were singled out for consideration, underlining their perceived importance relative to the type of care proposed.

'During her stay at the hostel, Shirley has appeared as a fairly high grade and comparatively capable person. It seems that she will be able to cope quite adequately in a group home situation. She is always cheerful, clean and tidy although she does need some guidance regarding hair and dress sometimes. It is difficult to determine from her behaviour, largely because of her passive nature, whether she actually likes a given situation or whether she simply accepts her position. She interacts fairly well with the other residents, although she does not have any special friends in the hostel. As far as her domestic capabilities are concerned, it seems likely that Shirley would be able to cope, relatively easily, with preparing her own meals, shopping and coping with her money.'

Four cases were found where the professional view questioned the desirability of the client ever having been admitted into hospital care. The 'subnormal' label was marked out as inappropriate and this appeared to justify the suitability of the present proposed alternative care.

'This woman is not subnormal. Her IQ is in the region of 100. She is in fact using a bed which could be filled many times over by a severely subnormal patient from the community.'
'Although labelled a subnormal, this is slight. She is able to do all her own washing and cleaning and is on the whole a very clean and tidy person.'

In one case a report stated the client in question 'behave(d) essentially as a normal member of the community but (was) homeless', emphasising the extent to which it was felt that the current form of 'care' was quite

105

inappropriate. Work attitude and ability were stressed several times, particularly in reporting on a person who had spent a long time in hospital: 'he's a good worker', 'she has worked very hard over the years', 'This is a severely subnormal man who has been for many years in hospital. He is an expert launderer and has, in the past, been able to do a full day's work ironing shirts etc.'. Sometimes however, favourable descriptions like these were accompanied by words like 'institutionalised' or 'used to routine' which have negative implications for being able to cope with a more independent lifestyle.

There was, furthermore, evidence of a short-term change in direction of professional opinion, for example, to take the case of Gladys. Shortly prior to her move from the ward to the domestic training unit within the hospital grounds, she was described in the following way by the Medical Consultant, 'She is severely subnormal in that her intelligence is under average and she is unable to lead an independent life. She is very slow and unlikely to hold down a job. . . . . A simple-minded cheerful woman who is quite capable but she is institutionalised and will never be able to live without supervision.' It must have come as a surprise later when the same person was able to write of her that she 'coped very well indeed, showed much independence and would probably be able to manage most everyday situations.'

(iii) *Training of residents in the homes*

Training and support given to residents following their move to the home covered several common areas — Social Work staff dealt with individual problem-solving, budgeting, and giving general advice; Home Helps were concered with housekeeping, which included shopping, room-cleaning, washing, ironing and mending clothes. The main problem concerned defining the relative responsibilities of individual staff which included the extent to which they should be involved in teaching residents to live more independently.

Home Help support

The whole question of the role and function of the Home Helps in the group homes requires careful analysis as the matter gave rise to a number of contentious issues. The overall problem concerned the lack of clarity regarding the tasks of Home Helps, their accountability to management and their relationships with the Social Workers. These aspects are interlinked but are to be dealt with separately in order to show which characteristics are associated with each different home.

(a) *The nature of their tasks:* It was not entirely clear what the background to this problem was — for example, were the Home Helps basically unwilling to cooperate in the achievement of the set goals, were they not fully aware of the perspective in which these goals had been set (in which case had their 'training' been adequate) or did they simply believe that the set goals were unrealistic?

There was evidence that they had felt unqualified for the roles expected of them:

'Mrs. S. is of the opinion that she and Mrs. A. have not received enough advice and support from, to quote 'the people with the expertise of dealing with subnormals'. They both feel this way apparently and say that apart from myself and occasional visits from the Divisional Officer and of course the Home Help Supervisor there has been no one.'

(Social Work Assistant)

'At the meeting Mrs. T. said that in her view the training that she and the other Home Help had received was inadequate and she went on to suggest 'that future Home Helps chosen for the group homes or residential work with the mentally handicapped should receive something better'.

(Principal Social Worker)

This led Home Helps to feel a sense of isolation from the core of the project and contributed to their resentment towards other staff. At GH2 her lack of training had been associated instead with the Home Help feeling more qualified than others to direct and supervise residents. Her argument was based on the fact that she had more day-to-day contact with the residents, hence she was more familiar with them and experienced in knowing their ways:

'23.2.76
Telephone call from Mrs. He. informing me she had had her 'phone connected at her new address. She talked for over ten minutes — the usual gist of the conversation being complaints. She complained that Mr. R. (Buildings Officer) had made a visit to (GH2) and that she wished he would keep away and stop promising to give them things they had been promised. She told me I had to go round and tell the girls they were not to use the electric fires as per Mr. R. (Buildings Officer). She said he also complained that we should have had the gas payment meter removed and the gas put on an account. Mrs. He. also complained about Violet taking money away from Susan and Beryl and said I shouldn't let the young ones be responsible for their own money. She also informed me that I was a fool for letting (the other Home Help) and the girls "blind me with science" over £5.00 for Doris for corsets. She said she had got her two pairs last year and she had cut them up. I informed her that Doris could have the corsets and if she cut them up it was her lookout, she would get no more if this was so. She told me I ought to tell (the other Home Help) not to let them have things. She complained also about the girls buying things out of their pocket money which she told them she would buy from housekeeping money.....'

(Social Work Assistant)

The residents themselves resented Mrs. He.'s intervention and her domineering attitude, according to the same diary:

107

'28.2.76
I saw Violet and Doris the other day. Both seemed reasonably happy apart from the usual moans about Mrs. He. not buying food they requested her to buy and shouting at them for minor things such as burning too much electricity and gas.'

There was further evidence of Home Helps showing too overprotective an attitude towards residents than that which was needed, indicating either a failure to grasp their role in pursuing the main goal of promoting resident independence or their denial of the practical and realistic nature of this role. The minutes of GH5 staff meetings provided several examples of the attitudes of Home Helps towards teaching residents tasks:

'Item — *Overprotection of residents: carving of meat*
(The Principal Social Worker) expressed concern that on his recent Sunday visits he had noticed that the lunchtime meat was already cut up. When questioned Lily Nichols had said that the Home Helps had cooked the meat on Saturday and then sliced it into small pieces so that all they had to do was heat it in the oven on Sunday for their lunch. Home Help claims that unless she followed this procedure residents might cut themselves. (Principal Social Worker) protested that unless the girls were given the opportunity they would never learn, and we must not over-protect them to such an extent. The danger of an accidental cut while carving the weekend joint was a calculated risk that we must take. Ms. P. (Home Help Organiser) at first supported the Home Helps' overcautious attitude but eventaully accepted that the Home Helps would henceforth supervise and train the residents to carve meat themselves.

Item — *Ironing*
(The Principal Social Worker) queried whether the residents did any ironing or whether this was also being done for them by the Home Helps. He said that the girls claimed their personal items like underwear were worn unironed and if this was the case he would like to hear the Home Helps' comments.
Mrs. R. (Home Help) said they had tried to supervise the girls in ironing without any success so they had ceased to bother. Underwear etc. was washed weekly and its cleanliness was more important than the lack of ironing.
(The Principal Social Worker) had accepted this but pointed out he had made a number of enquiries among a wide range of females seeking their views about this. . . . . (general feeling was that) ironed underwear was desired by all.
(The Principal Social Worker) suggested that if this is the attitude of 'normal people' then surely if we are pursuing the accepted goal of 'normalisation' for the (GH5) residents we must inculcate the practice with them. . . . .
The Home Helps suggested that the girls who could iron wouldn't and the others were too clumsy not to be 'at risk'. (The Principal Social Worker) commented that all the girls had received hospital O.T. training in ironing so

108

he would be surprised if any were seriously at risk. Nevertheless they must all be encouraged to follow a regular routine of doing their own ironing whenever possible. If any problems were encountered or any resident refused then the Home Helps must report back and the (Principal) or (Social Work Assistant) would take it up with the individual concerned'.

The Home Helps in this case only partially come round to accepting their teaching role for a division of opinion still existed between them and Social Work staff regarding the relative abilities of residents and the appropriateness of this type of individual goal setting. They received verbal support from the Home Help Organiser whose views indicated that she also perceived the residents, first and foremost, in terms of their need for care and practical support. This whole business had reached something of a climax for the Area Officer to have become eventually involved. In a meeting he suggested that each support worker in turn 'review the past and current situation at the home', following which he attempted, as overall manager, to define the functions of both Home Help and Social Work inputs.

'Mrs. T. (Home Help) was ambivalent but believed some ongoing supervisoin would always be needed.
Ms. P. (Home Help Organiser) said she had always had the impression that the hospital staff resented the Home Helps' involvement and she had not expected there would be any social work needs by the (GH5) residents. If any arose she was under the impression that her two nominated Home Helps would deal with the problems.
Mrs. R. (Home Help) believed there had been a big improvement in residents' behaviour and that they were getting better all the time.
Mr. W. (Home Help Organiser) was critical about the lack of social work involvement in the early stages of (GH5).
Mr. F. (Principal Social Worker) agreed with Ps. P. that there was some resentment from hospital staff who had put in a lot of time and effort to prepare the initial intake of residents only to be informed by the Department that as a matter of policy their involvement should cease once the girls took up residence.....Mr. F. shared Mrs. R.'s opinion that the residents had shown some improvement but he also believed that this improvement should have been achieved a lot sooner. Overprotectiveness despite its good intentions was the chief factor in the delay. Although Mrs. T. could possibly be right in her view that they would always require ongoing supervision, the only way in which it could be proven was by putting the girls to the test and to refrain from doing things for them. Regarding the introduction of (the Social Work Assistant) in her role as welfare assistant to (GH5), this step was a logical development after the need for such assistance became apparent. Her escorting residents to and from the Gateway Club, for shopping expeditions, visits to the GP etc. were essential. It often entailed evening and weekend visits when the Home Help was not on duty. In fact (the Social Work Assistant's) role was complimentary, not an overlapping non-essential one to that of the Home Helps.'

The Area Officer stated that the job of the Home Helps was 'to train the residents in domestic and household skills' and mentioned, for example, cooking, cleaning, use of domestic appliances, shopping and budgeting for food and that 'the social work service would deal with such things as personal savings, spendings (clothing etc.), holidays, leisure activities, escorts to doctors and others and residents' problems at work or at the training centre'. From this point onwards Home Helps began in principle to abide by the set goal of teaching residents to become more independent.

'Their (the Home Help Service) argument for retaining three days' attendance weekly was based on the need for fresh vegetable purchases. We conceded the point on the understanding that the residents were given an opportunity to do this for themselves.'
'As from next week in accordance with our treatment goal Home Help Services will be withdrawn on Wednesdays. The residents are to do their own mid-week shopping on that day on a rota basis with a list made out on Mondays by the Home Helps.'
'The Home Helps are now allowing the residents to do some purchasing of provisions from local tradesmen and (the Social Work Assistant) has visited the shops most frequently used and obtained the owners' cooperation towards our treatment goals. The shopkeeper will countersign the shopping lists tendered by the residents but will also help with our future intentions for the residents to shop verbally with the shopkeeper writing down the order and pricing of each item.'

The minutes of these meetings stated that the original GH5 Home Helps had been redeployed and replaced by another pair who had been consigned to a 'special training course'. This had provided an opportunity to set out formally the hours worked by the Home Helps and to specify, within limits, their tasks.

(b) *Their perception of tasks:* Data gathered from the staff interviews provided a range of individual perspectives on the role of Home Helps and illustrate the complications that emerged. The following relates to GH1 and describes the initial Home Help service provided to residents in the words of the Home Help Staff.

Area Home Help Organiser
'Home Helps went in seven days per week. They trained the girls in bulk shopping, budgeting, ironing, washing and cleaning the house. They started off a rota for them. The Home Help was taking two of the girls to work early in the morning, making sure the girls got up and were breakfasted. Their hours were 7–9 a.m., 5–7 p.m. There was only one Home Help at any one time in the home, though at the beginning both were there to deal with the shopping and other things. There was all-intensive Home Help input for six months.'

District Home Help Organiser
'The Home Helps helped the residents in money handling, budgeting, menu planning, shopping, laundering, cooking and general home organisation. We

told the Home Helps they were supposed to be supportive. They weren't to do the jobs for them.'

Home Help (1)

'We were asked to take them to work, organise their meals, and shopping. We had to make sure they knew how to get to the shops. We were told how to deal with their meals and the cleaning of the house. It was more automatic. We were told to teach them. We did everything together. We chose one of the five to be housekeeper. We did it for the first week or two then we got them to take over and so we supervised.'

Home Help (2)

'We escorted them to work, taught them how to cook, clean, how to shop and to budget.'

In the above case, there would seem to have been little if any confusion concerning the appropriate role of the Home Helps — they were asked to assist residents in their learning of certain skills and by and large, this appears to have been accomplished relatively successfully. The position relating to the teaching function of Home Helps elsewhere, in particular at GH2 and 6, was not so clear and these are singled out below for illustration.

Although the residents at GH2 received support from both Social Work and Home Help staff after moving into the home, the evidence indicated that this had not been directed specifically towards enabling residents to become more independent. Though some attempts had been made to teach skills, these had not on the whole been very successful. The overall impression was one of confusion regarding the exact role and function of, in particular, Home Help support. Whereas it was recognised that very little had actually been achieved in terms of enabling residents to survive independently, it was not altogether clear whether this had been due to a failure on the part of support staff directly involved or to the absence of a satisfactory operational policy among support staff that was clearly aimed at reducing the demand for support services. It had been recognised that, at the beginning, prior to the involvement of any of the current support staff, a nurse from the local mental handicap hospital had tried to teach residents some basic household skills. Soon after, Home Help (1) had become involved while at this time the group home was still technically under the auspices of the West Riding Local Authority. This prior involvement of Home Help (1) seemed to account in part for the relatively unsatisfactory state of affairs that had emerged in which no single officer was prepared to make such basic innovations in the organisation of the home that would be consistent with the need to match formal support to the overall needs of residents.

111

(What preparation/training for independent living did the resident receive *after* moving to the home?)

Area Officer

'Very little. We've been trying to persuade the Home Helps to allow them to be independent.'

Princial Social Worker

'Not provide this as such. A lot of day-to-day help is given by the Social Work Assistants and the Home Helps but residents are rather cossetted if anything.'

Specialist Social Worker

'Home Help visits. This was training in cooking mostly as most hospital patients are OK at housekeeping. They were given a programme on how to deal with this on a rota basis.'

Social Work Assistant

'There was first a nurse at the home then a gradual takeover in support from her to Mrs. He. (Home Help (1)) so that at one time she was the only person involved.'

Area Home Help Organiser

'It is the Home Helps' function to make the residents independent. The Home Help hours have varied. At the beginning: Home Help support *everyday*, two people each 2 hours per day. At present Mrs. He. is five hours daily (Monday-Friday) and Mrs. Ho. is two hours daily (Monday-Thursday) and weekends (sometimes four hours daily). The hours have not been reduced. My assumption is that the Home Helps have never been trained. When I first found out about it I reduced the hours, that is two years ago but only reduced the weekend work. But I've found it difficult; if you train someone to do a job you'll eventually do yourself out of a job. I've put it to the Area Officer but received no support. We have been told by the Home Helps that the clients are low grade and so they'll always need them. So what can I do? It is difficult. Who assesses the client? It is not my job. My argument is that they're doing the same thing now as in 1976.

However since 1976 I've been getting Mrs. He. to list things she does every week. But it's the same this year as the last, e.g. "seeing to things", "giving them tablets", "doing the shopping". I can offer them other work in the vicinity but they say they've enough work there and I can't assess the grade of handicap. I'm told the clients are very bad. I can't simply get rid of Mrs. He. or reduce her hours without her cooperation otherwise she'll get the union on me. If the Social Work side came to me and said the residents don't need the support they're getting then with proof I could reduce the Home Help hours. But this was tried and we let them do the shopping alone, but they got in a mess, lifted things and I was proved wrong. Mrs. He. said "I told you so". I mean the Social Work side haven't come to me to support this much, although I want to reduce the hours. It's no good if you're trying to make them independent. There's not enough liaison. I don't know what she's (Mrs. He.) doing half the time. There's no feedback. As for the Group Home Meetings we're not invited are we, I should be. We're not told anything. I think the Social Work side should give me support. She (Mrs. He.) was told when she started the job that she would be there forever. Even if I proved she was an incompetent teacher I still couldn't get rid of her as I'd have the union on me.'

District Home Help Organiser

'Home Help teaching. Mrs. He. was established before I was involved so I am not aware of what she was told. After 1974 (Local Government reorganisation) we tried to encourage Mrs. He. to teach but unsuccessfully so we passed it back to the Social Work Department. Up to 1974 Mrs. He. was not classified as Home Help staff but part of the Social Work side and we had to establish our control over her.'

Home Help (1)

'It was assumed that basic training had been completed before they moved in permanently, before I took over. Then there was nothing systematic, for example, if they had a problem, I taught them how to deal with it. I basically don't have time to teach properly as they're so institutionalised, for example, there's the washer, they won't use it as it should be used. I've had two or three morning sessions doing it properly while I'm there but when I've gone they revert back to their own way. Also beds, they get up, the house is cold, it's instilled in them, they've got to make their beds hospital-wise. My idea is that they get up and have a warm breakfast then they do the beds. They do it like that when I'm there but not when I'm not. Also their tablets. The idea was to give them out at set times in hospital so that no one got missed out. They take them at mealtimes whether they need them or not just as if in hospital. I grieved over my hours being chopped. At first I was doing everything, evenings too. Then I suggested that Mrs. Ho. participate as she was involved informally already. At that time I was doing everyday. Now twenty-two hours only.'

Home Help (2)

'Training from Home Helps. Not formal. We did things voluntarily such as teaching them to prepare meals and see that their clothes matched.'

Side by side with the apparent failure to teach skills to residents was the fact that no proper efforts had been made by the back-up members of the support team either to encourage the Home Helps to play a more effective teaching role or to initiate them directly in the particular teaching qualities required. There was a resistance on the part of Mrs. He. towards having her involvement with the home lessened, which in itself implied a basic reluctance to make the residents less dependant on her. It was particularly significant to note the attitude of Mrs. He.'s senior officer: she felt her "hands tied" in relation to limiting the degree of involvement Mrs. He. had with the home. She could not simply, by her own authority, reduce Mrs. He.'s working hours unless a separate authorisation had been received from the Area Officer as overall administrative head. The argument has been presented that this could have been done on the grounds that the current support input to the home was not facilitating the achievement of the goals set for it. However, the general conclusion would be that no more than lip-service had been paid to setting goals of independence and suchlike for residents for anything more than this would have entailed a greater degree of organisation and communication within the support team than that which existed.

The main variation in answers given by GH6 staff also concerned this difficult question of the actual role of Home Help support. Whereas most other staff stated that some training had been provided by the Home Helps the Home Helps themselves denied that this was the case. The 'official' view was that Home Helps had taught residents a range of skills, for example, cooking, shopping, ironing and that on one day a week they had stayed at home specifically for this purpose. However, the Home Helps stated that it had not been possible to carry out any training. In fact their answers suggested that they had been unclear of the real purpose of training in the sense intended.

Home Help (1)

'There was nothing specific laid down as far as I know. They needed a bit of coaxing to do things for themselves. I used to get them to hoover up and that. We were told to help them, to teach them to do things for themselves so as they could live on their own eventually. If I stood over them they'd do the job. When they were out I'd get through jobs myself quickly. I felt terrible asking them to do things as I thought that was my job.'

Home Help (2)

'Very little. We were told at the beginning that our job was to teach them to do domestic jobs and shopping for themselves. But no further advice was given. How do you teach an illiterate to shop? I was sent on a training course but after that I was taken out of the home. The training course helped me do things, simplify things, but I was not given a chance to put these things into operation.'

(C) Their accountability to management

A main problem facing GH2 and 5 had been the inconclusive arrangement regarding who had authority over the Home Helps. The overall position was indisputable insofar as the Area Officer had administrative responsibility but the managerial level below that had been less clear: were Home Helps directly accountable to one or other of their Supervisors or to one of the Social Work staff, and if so, which one? Were they in the first instance accountable to their Supervisor but in terms of overall management to the Principal Social Worker? Indeed, were they really accountable to anyone?

GH2 provided perhaps the strongest example of this type of administrative confusion, illustrated through the Department's failure to adequately monitor the activities of the Home Helps. The Social Work 'diary' showed numerous instances of Mrs. He.'s difficult attitude — her sharp criticism of individual residents for disobeying her, her dominant temperament, her deviousness, her total refusal to play a secondary role — 'I couldn't tell her what to do, I just had to listen to her moans, one after the other.' (Social Work Assistant).

In the early days of GH5 the phased withdrawal of Home Helps had been a problem for Social Work staff to contend with. The minutes of group meetings showed how certain staff felt unsure about their right to make decisions affecting the integrity of the scheme and particularly insofar as this related to the management of Home Helps.

'The Area Home Help Organiser claimed she was unaware of the recent decision to withdraw future Home Help services during the evenings and on Saturdays. (The Principal Social Worker) explained that the decision had been taken only after consultation with (the Area Officer) and therefore a failure in communication was apparent. A phased withdrawal of Home Help services had been implicit from the very beginning of the (GH5) project, after all it was basic to the entire concept of maximising the individual and collective abilities of the resident's potential to enable them to function at a minimum dependency level.

Comment:

There does seem an undoubted reluctance on part of the Home Helps to reduce their hours of involvement at (GH5). The idea of working themselves out of employment so to speak is unacceptable — hence their approach to (AHHO) about the impracticability of curtailing current high support levels. The problem is tricky in the managerial sense and will need rather delicate handling to achieve the cooperation without bruising their feelings. (AHHO) is not so well at present and so it is inopportune to tell her that her choice of Home Helps is a poor one. How can we possibly gauge the residents' abilities to cope unaided if everything is being done for them.'

It had become clear to Social Work Staff that 'the initial choice of Home Helps was ill-judged' — 'for quite unknown reasons they have retarded the residents' progress and seriously delayed our projected treatment goals...' — yet, at that stage, it was not so clear whether in fact the Principal Social Worker had direct authority to remove them out of the home.

'It is difficult to raise this critical indictment with (AHHO) too forcibly as both these Home Helps were specially selected by her and criticism of them is a criticism of her.'

With support from the Area Officer, the Principal Social Worker managed to get the situation changed and new Home Helps were found. However, judging from the file data, ensuing cooperation between the two services became henceforth conducted, on the Home Help side, with the DHHO (District Home Help Organiser), despite the AHHO's continued attendance at group meetings. Arrangements for the hours and working conditions of the new Home Helps were openly discussed at meetings, and although the AHHO still maintained opposition to substantial Home Help withdrawal, her comments went largely ignored. On the thorny question of accountability, the position had been straightened:

'(Principal Social Worker) said that in the ultimate matter of accountability for anything connected with (GH5) he was prepared to accept full responsibility. As the Area Officer had delegated authority to him in respect of (GH5), (Principal Social Worker) believed therefore that he himself should be the accountable person.'

(d) Their relationship with Social Workers and with each other: The problem here mainly consisted of a failure by Home Help staff to fully appreciate the role of Social Work in the homes, and resulted from the overall ambiguity characterising their own role. At GH1 and 5 Home Helps had borne resentment towards the Social Work Staff for what they perceived as having their role taken over in the home and, furthermore, for the latter's failure to adequately recognise the part Home Helps played in initially 'socialising' residents. The GH1 'diary' recorded how the Home Helps appeared hostile to having their position ousted — 'they said that they'd not been given notice of our decision to take them out of the home and they naturally felt very resentful' (Social Work Assistant) — partly because they had become very attached to the residents in the earlier stages when the latter had received far more intensvie support.

The position had been similar at GH5 where Home Helps had carried the burden of support earlier on and had resolved the many practical problems that had arisen. The AHHO had thought that Home Helps would deal with the 'social work needs' of residents and this belief of hers that Home Helps would play the key support role was naturally transmitted down to her workers. The prior involvement in the home of Mrs. He. at GH2 had largely accounted for her persistent stubbornness in meeting the demands of Social Work staff. In summary, their failure to perceive correctly the social work role in the homes, the feeling on the part of Home Helps that their prior involvement deserved greater recognition and the endorsement of their view by their Supervisors all contributed to their having a fairly negative attitude towards any kind of social work intervention.

Disagreements were not often openly displayed by the parties concerned, although it was clear that certain Home Helps did harbour grievances against each other. Sometimes these were sufficiently serious to affect the overall provision of support. One clear example concerned the different attitudes held by Home Helps towards the residents of the group. At GH2 there was a marked difference of attitude between the Home Helps: one acted strictly towards the residents, spending money as fastidiously as possible and tending to impose her own rather severe standards on them; the other was far more lenient, granting them much freedom in their activities.

The Social Work Assistant tried to mediate, but, in effect, tended to consciously resist the oppressive influence of the first Home Help. 'She always "skimps" with them in buying clothing and everything, as though

116

she's spending her own money'. She considered that the Home Help went too far in imposing her standards, in criticising how residents spent their personal monies and how they pursued their leisure activities, for example, Beryl's embroidery. 'I told you to do each of those flowers a different colour, not the same'. At times such incidents caused difficulties, for if this Home Help found that residents were behaving contrary to the plans set for them, she would immediately report the incident to the Social Work Assistant who would be expected to take action. For example, she reported that residents were being 'devious' — 'they rush through their work in the morning and as soon as I've gone, on goes the TV, but they know when I'm returning in the afternoon like I do sometimes and it's always off in time.'

At GH4 there had been a difficult situation from the outset: the Home Helps never made contact with one another as they visited the home at different times and neither of them made official contact with the visiting Social Worker. One Home Help considered that her efforts to teach residents to budget in buying food were in vain as she claimed that the other Home Help would spend the remaining housekeeping money more freely. Both Home Helps considered that the Social Worker's notion of teaching residents to become independent was ill-founded. They felt that the group was unresponsive to teaching and that the whole excercise was 'a waste of time'. 'When I try to tell them about cooking and how they must wash up their dishes and put them away, they don't listen, it doesn't sink in, they're not interested. I tell them to put the crocks to soak in hot water but they just leave them there in cold water, they don't listen.' One Home Help resented the Social Worker for treating her 'as the lowest of the low': she felt that the Social Worker was not prepared to discuss with her her role and the general aims set for the home. As a result she felt undervalued and this feeling was enhanced following both Home Helps' sudden removal from the home.

In a further home, GH6, the Home Help considered that the chosen residents were 'unsuitable' for various reasons and this strength of feeling revealed resentment towards Social Work Staff for having selected them in the first place. She criticised one resident for his meanness, idleness and lack of cooperation. He was extremely reluctant to spend any of his private money: he would hoard food, take more than his fair share and act with little, if any, consideration towards his fellow resident. He was idle: the Home Help complained of how he refused to attend 'work', would lie around all day getting in her way, would expect her to prepare a lunch for him at his request and would not make any effort to assist her. She tended to be more sympathetic with the other less obstinate, more placid resident, although she stated that his withdrawn personality made him fundamentally unsuitable for the home.

(iii) Summary: Comments made in the files of individual clients by professional staff prior to the move to a group home had often been

recommendations for a group home placement and had emphasised social competence and personality traits. They had placed a special emphasis on ability to cater for basic self-care needs and to accomplish household tasks. It had also been recognised by staff that certain clients deserved community placement since they ought never to have been in hospital or diagnosed as mentally handicapped in the first instance. The files had shown evidence of change in the professional assessments of individual clients from those where the client had been described as 'too handicapped' or 'institutionalised' to those where he had been acknowledged in terms suggesting him as a suitable group home candidate.

To summarise on this whole issue of Home Help support, the argument has been presented that there were three main sides to the problem: the nature of tasks, accountability to management and the interface with social work. The first of these had been the crux of the total problem — the tasks and orientation of Home Helps had not been adequately spelled out and where they had there had been reluctance to undertake the type of role envisaged. Homes Helps had felt unqualified for this type of role, though in one contrasting case the Home Help felt more than qualified owing to her earlier involvement. They had resented being ousted and complained over the inadequate support and lack of information that they had received. The first problem had been compounded by the failure to provide proper official administrative accountability for Home Helps, which had led to confusion on the part of other staff in relating to them. In one case, a rational decision to have Home Helps withdrawn could not initially be implemented owing to the entrenched opposition of the Home Help Supervisor in her refusal to actively support social work goals of promoting resident independence.

Where there had been resentment by the Home Help service towards social work intervention, this had been due mainly to its failure to appreciate the role of social work, the prescribed needs of residents and the overall orientation of the scheme. Home Helps had resented their treatment from Social Work staff who had not given them adequate recognition for all the work they had put in. They felt that Social Workers had misconceived the needs of residents, particularly insofar as the Home Helps had either stated or implied that they themselves offered the more appropriate type of support to residents. Furthermore, they had developed good friendly relationships with residents which, in their view, had been damaged following their sudden withdrawal. In overall terms, the data indicated the wide gap between the two services in terms of the communication they had with one another and the service perspectives they employed.

SECTION 3 — Administration and Operation of Policy

(i) Decision-making

The data showed that few examples existed of formal decision-making bodies for any of the group homes. Each home's experience on this matter differed and throughout no clear-cut model of decision-making emerged.

Staff of two homes acknowledged the existence of 'group home meetings' though their role and function were not the same in each case. At GH5 they constituted a recognisable decision-making group involving all relevant support workers below the level of Area Officer. This group dealt with a wide range of home-related matters and consulted the Area Officer only when they were unable to reach an agreement. In the other case, GH2 meetings involved the participation of direct care staff plus the Principal Social Worker but their administrative status in relation to the formation of policy was not clear. For the other homes staff acknowledged the existence of ad-hoc decision-making arrangements to deal with specific policy matters. For example, at GH1 and 4 meetings were held to decide upon prospective residents, at GH3 there was at least one inter-agency meeting to discuss preliminary arrangements for the home, and similarly at GH6, there were several meetings to determine early policy.

The information obtained suggested that most decision-making was informally-based, involving often no more than two support workers attached to a home. In several instances, when asked to state their contacts with other staff, a contact was recognised by one party without it being reciprocated by the relevant other. Set channels of inter-staff communication evolved for each home and in this regard, the coordinative function of particular individuals became gradually established. In GH1 for example, the Principal Social Worker was the 'link man' between the Area Officer and the Social Work Assistant at the home level and between the Social Work and Home Help support 'teams'; in GH4 the Social Worker played a central role, being involved in all decision-making relating to support provision and in GH5 a similar part was played by the Principal Social Worker. The contacts between Social Worker and Home Help staff varied considerably in relation to each home, but usually they were made through a single representative of each staff group.

Respondents from GH5 stated that their meetings usually took place monthly but these had recently become less frequent — main discussion topics being the nature of Home Help support, progress and health of residents and general household matters. At GH2 there was a discrepancy between the views of staff regarding the function of their somewhat irregular meetings. The Principal Social Worker described it as an opportunity for staff to 'ventilate' their problems, whereas direct care staff saw its function in more positive terms — to implement 'general changes to the home', to deal with behaviour problems of residents, to discuss the need for new equipment, clothing and furniture.

Some meetings took place in the early stages of a home's development — at GH1 and 4 references were made to meetings to determine and assess resident intake that sometimes involved staff other than those currently providing support. Such staff included the Senior Medical Consultant, a hostel principal and training centre managers. Similarly at GH6 there were references to an 'earlier group concerned with running the home' that involved the Area Officer, the Specialist Social Worker (Mental Handicap), the Departmental Assessments Officer (Finance), the Principal Assistant (Mental Health) and the Area Home Help Organiser. The Principal Social Worker at GH3 summarised a first meeting that took place between representatives from his department and hospital staff:

'The first issue was that we agreed on who would be responsible for what. We offered financial aid, community integration, social work support. The hospital seemed to feel that it was not necessary but we agreed to do this bit anyway. Basically the hospital was responsible for everything. They would keep in contact on a regular basis. As for social work involvement we said we would provide a social worker if they asked for one.'

From this it seemed that the meeting made some attempt to clarify the roles of respective agencies. According to another respondent, further meetings took place in the early stages at the home itself involving the Social Worker and one or more of the hospital staff.

There was often a marked difference in the type and amount of decision-making seen to exist in relation to each home by the different staff concerned. At GH1 the Principal Social Worker specified his involvement in both formal and informal decision-making with a range of other staff; the Social Work Assistant mainly referred to her routine consultations with the Principal when she would sometimes seek advice as to how to handle problem situations; on the Home Help side there was little recognition of any organised decision-making — both Home Helps stated that they knew of no decison-making situations and the Area and District Organisers merely acknowledged a mutual decision-making arrangement 'to discuss Home Help involvement'.

The example of GH2 is as follows, illustrating individual staff perceptions of the existence of both formal and informal decision-making.

Area Officer

'(1) Home Helps with their Organiser and the one above that.
(2) Specialist Social Worker + Social Work Assistant + Principal Social Worker
(3) Area Officer with overall control as a decision-maker.
(4) Admin. side: Admin. Assistant + Assessments Officer.
(5) Higher Admin. side: (example of cases involving) the Deputy Director.'

Principal Social Worker

'(1) Principal Social Worker + Specialist Social Worker + Social Work Assistant is one decision-making body.
(2) Meetings with all staff at the GH2 home itself.

120

(3) At a higher level: Area Officer/Administrative Assistant in relation to matters such as finance.

(4) At even higher level: Central Administration — telephones, money matters, buildings.

Specialist Social Worker

'Group home meetings involving the Social Work Assistant, Principal Social Worker, Specialist Social Worker and Home Helps.'

Social Work Assistant

'Group home staff meetings, every month, usually more infrequent. I make most of the decisions in cooperation with the Home Helps.'

Area Home Help Organiser

'Home Help decision-making group; the Area Home Help Organiser plus the two Home Helps, only informal, if there are any problems'.

District Home Help Organiser

'I don't know really. I'm not involved much in decision-making apart from duties and hours of Home Helps.'

Home Help (1)

'Group home meetings.'

Home Help (2)

'Group home meetings.'

There was a rather clear contrast between the perceptions of staff at the client interface level and those of staff at a more administrative level of the hierarchy. The former referred solely to the group home meetings whereas the latter indicated the existence of other types of administrative and supervisory arrangement. This was a noticeable overall characteristic and underlined the hierarchical differences relating to staff involvement in policy and further differences emerging from the division and relative status of Social Work and Home Help staff.

The following charts show how day-to-day problems emanating from the homes were referred upwards from one officer to his senior. In cases involving both Social Work and Home Help staff, the usual procedure was for a Home Help to refer a matter to the Social Worker or Assistant rather than upwards direct to her senior officer.

For GH1 initial arangement was different from the present one insofar as the former involved the Home Help service. Both Home Help Organisers stated that the residents took their problems to either or both Home Helps who referred them on to the Organiser(s) if they were unable to deal with them. Referral was then made by either or both Organisers to the Principal Social Worker if they considered it necessary. The Home Helps stated in contradiction, however, that they referred problem matters directly to the Principal Social Worker, only approaching their Organiser(s) when the former was unavailable. The present arrangement can be illustrated as follows:

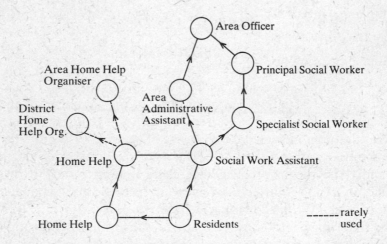

For GH2 the day-to-day decision-making method can be show by the following diagrammatic form:

For GH3 the initial arrangement was for the residents to contact either the Specialist Social Worker or a member of staff at the hospital if they had any problems they could not handle. If necessary, the Social Worker referred the matter upwards for advice from his senior (the Principal Social Worker in this case). The current arrangement was for residents either to refer a matter to the Nursing Assistant who, in some cases, proceeded to refer it upwards to her senior officer at the hospital, or for them to refer it directly to a member of staff at the hospital.

For GH4 the initial procedure was as follows:

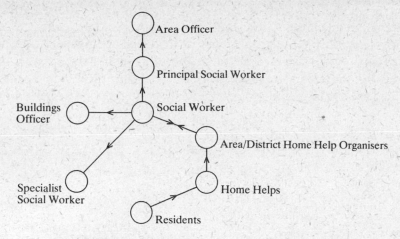

Throughout at GH5 the procedure could be broadly seen as:

In the above case, in distinguishing between whether the Home Helps referred a matter to their senior officer(s) or to the Social Work Assistant, it seemed that referral to the former was made in relation to 'work' or 'duty' matters and to the latter in relation to matters concerned with 'the welfare of residents'.

Finally, the initial arrangement at GH6 involved the Home Help service and is illustrated in the following chart (see overleaf). The later arrangement, following the removal of the Home Helps, meant that residents referred matters to either the Specialist Social Worker or the Social Work Assistant.

(ii) *Treatment of residents*

The majority of residents under retiring age were already attending a training centre or in open employment at the time of their move to the group home and remained there such that support workers did not become involved in decisions regarding placement. Where the need did arise, for example at GH2, the task was the responsibility of the member of Social Work staff in closest daily contact with the home. At GH5 decisions were made by the Social Work Assistant in consultation with the

Principal Social Worker. With regard to the monitoring of individual residents, in all cases it was clear that no formal arrangements existed in terms of establishing set goals. Several informal arrangements occurred but these only consisted of the reporting of incidents and changes in the homes by direct care staff to senior officials. In GH1 and 5 this was claimed to have been undertaken regularly during supervision sessions; in

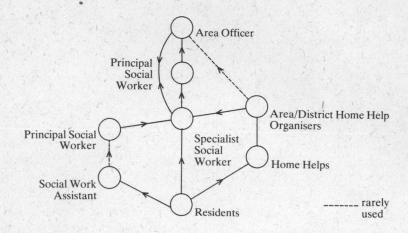

GH2 and 5 the group home meeting was the medium through which such reporting was also done, and in other cases the formal six monthly client review applied.

Residents in official retirement were left to devise their own work and leisure activities though advice and help was sometimes given. At GH2 the Social Work Assistant established a contact with a local day centre which residents began to attend on a weekly basis. In other cases where residents were not employed a referral was made by the Social Work person involved to the Work Assessment Unit whereupon the client was assessed and subsequently placed in a local training centre.

(iii) *Staffing support*

Initial decisions to determine the amount of staff support needed for the homes were made by the relevant Area Officers in consultation with others, for example, Principal Social Workers and Area Home Help Organisers. The actual selection of direct care staff was normally delegated to the Principal Social Worker in relation to social work support and the Area and/or District Home Help Organiser in relation to Home Help support. In the case of at least three homes, it appears to have been assumed that the Area Specialist Social Worker (Mental Handicap) would automatically be involved. There was little, if any, evidence of direct monitoring and assessment of staff input to the homes. On the social work side, Social Workers and Assistants were 'monitored' in the regular supervision sessions held with their senior officers but this was not undertaken in a structured way. At GH2 Home Helps completed weekly timesheets which were submitted to their senior officers specifying the nature of daily tasks but, in this case at any rate, the Area Home Help Organiser had no independent authority to make changes to working hours. At GH5 several staff mentioned the 'monitoring' function of the group home meetings but these appear to have concentrated their efforts on reducing Home Help support rather than appraising the need for support services as a whole. Finally, there have been few changes in staffing personnel (Table 4), the principal one being in relation to the withdrawal of Home Help support, although in the case of GH5 and 6 Home Helps have been withdrawn and others recruited.

There was evidence suggesting that decisions to determine the initial amount of staffing support required were made arbitrarily or else for good practical reasons, not least of which was associated with the needs of the group home. In one home, while still uninformed about the actual needs of the residents, the Area Home Help Organiser began by 'assum(ing) from the outset that the girls could do very little for themselves. We went through the week, going through all the events that would occur and took account of what would be needed assuming all the time that they would need help with almost everything'. In a later home set up by the same Area team the Home Help service was initially reluctant to become involved at all, and in all cases it was clear that Areas had not been allocated extra resources for group home schemes, hence it had been left to Home Help Organisers to decide on the amount of support they could afford to provide given alternative demands on their resources.

In selecting direct care staff, several factors were seen to be important. In two instances, staff lived in the same road which proved exceptionally valuable, though in fact they had already built up friendly contacts with residents prior to being appointed on an official basis. As regards some of the Home Helps, Area Organisers reported the difficulties in finding staff who were willing to work flexible hours, though in fairness, in relation to the selection of both Social Work and Home Help staff, certain homes had recognised the need to ensure that 'the right person(s)' should be appointed. As regards monitoring staff input, evidence showed how some social work staff worked relatively independently of their senior officials which has implications for the value of supervision received. In one home, the Social Worker reported that Home Helps were removed from the home following her recommendation on the grounds that she understood that residents had managed to learn an acceptable number of skills.

(iv) *Finances of residents*

Residents' finances were handled by different support workers depending on the group home in question. Both Social Work and Home Help staff were involved in the collection and distribution of monies and the payment of bills. GH3 differed markedly from the others as residents

Table 4   Turnover of staff (managerial and direct care)

Name of group home	Staff involved in providing support at beginning	Staff recruited	Staff departed	Present staff complement (Jan. 1979)
GH1	AO PSW AHHO DHHO HH(1) HH(2)	SWA	AHHO DHHO HH(1) HH(2)	AO PSW SWA
GH2	Unclear as under auspices of West Riding Authority. (Indications are that nurse(s) from OH4 were initially involved closely followed soon afterwards by HH(1)) AO PSW SW(sp.) SWA AHHO DHHO HH(2)	AO PSW SW(sp.) SWA AHHO DHHO HH(2)	SW(sp.)	AO PSW SWA AHHO DHHO HH(1) HH(2)
GH3	Range of OH2 hospital staff at Nursing Officer, Charge Nurse/Ward Sister and lower officer levels. AO PSW SW(sp.)	NA	AO	NA (with support from senior officer(s) at OH2)
GH4	AO PSW SW(sp.) AHHO DHHO HH(1) HH(2)		SW(sp.) AHHO DHHO HH(1) HH(2)	AO PSW
GH5	AO PSW(1) SWA AHHO DHHO HH(1) HH(2)	PSW(2) HH(3) HH(4)	PSW(1) HH(1) HH(2)	AO PSW(2) SWA AHHO DHHO HH(3) HH(4)
GH6	AO PSW SW(sp.) AHHO DHHO HH(1)	SWA HH(2) HH(3)	AHHO DHHO HH(1) HH(2) HH(3)	AO PSW SW(sp.) SWA

Key:
AO = Area Officer
AHHO = Area Home Help Organiser
DHHO = District Home Help Organiser
HH = Home Help

NA = Nursing Assistant
PSW = Principal Social Worker
SW = Social Worker
SWA = Social Work Assistant

handled almost all their finances independent of outside help. The majority of the remainder showed signs of moving towards more resident independence in financial matters judging from the changes that had taken place. One trend was the initial involvement of Home Helps in dealing with residents' finances, which in the case of GH1, 4 and 6 was related to the overall decision made at Area level to lessen Home Help support. In the majority of cases residents' incomes were divided up into amounts for maintenance such as rent and fuel, for housekeeping for personal expenditure and in some instances for personal savings.

The management of these allocations differed for each home reflecting the level of independence granted to residents. For example, at GH1, 3, 4 and 5 residents drew their weekly incomes themselves; at GH3 one resident had been delegated to collect maintenance and housekeeping payments from the others and these transactions were carried out and bills were paid without the need for outside help; at GH1 and 4 residents individually handed over amounts for maintenance to the Social Work support person, retaining the remainder for housekeeping and personal expenses; at GH5 residents handed over their total income to the Social Work Assistant who made the appropriate allocations forthwith. At GH2 and 6 the Social Work support person had been named appointee for the receipt of residents' incomes. In the two homes where Home Helps had been permanently involved, the Social Work Assistant paid over to them a set weekly amount for housekeeping, and to each resident a further amount for personal expenses. Cash returns were completed by Social Workers, stipulating the amounts received from individual residents and the allocations for various items, and these were then sent up to the Assessments Section of the Department where residents' private accounts were maintained.

(v) *Social and recreational activities of residents*

There were no explicit policies formulated regarding the provision of social and recreational activities of group home residents. The most common view expressed by support workers was that they should assist residents to develop their own social life rather than impose one on them. This was done either by informing residents of particular social events and facilitating their attendance at them, or in a more limited way, by responding positively to any independent initiative taken by one or more residents regarding a social event. Staff differed in their views, however, on the extent to which they believed that there was a policy or unwritten understanding concerning their involvement in the social lives of residents for each group home.

There were few examples of actual provisions made: at GH2, 3 and 5 there was a standing invitation to local hospital social functions, at GH6 the Social Worker introduced specific residents to local social clubs and at

GH1 and 4 staff initiated and took part in the occasional evening outing. In the main staff considered it important that residents should enjoy some kind of social life but that their role should be merely an enabling one. There were natural differences of opinion held by staff of particular homes, for in certain cases it was clear that staff believed that they should be taking a much more responsible role in creating opportunities for residents. Home Helps, in particular, took the view that, at least in the initial stages, support workers should have taken a more positive role — 'more should have been done as they sit here doing nothing'. Because of the geographical isolation of one home, the Social Worker and the Social Work Assistant agreed to make a conscious effort to encourage residents to use local facilities. Perhaps the general official view can be neatly summed up by quoting one Area Officer — 'Our objective is to provide information, encouragement and support to residents in seeking their own social and recreational pursuits. We don't 'lay on' specific activities for them. We give help in certain arrangements concerning holidays and day-trips.'

(vi) *Maintenance and equipment of homes*

A fairly uniform pattern emerged on how decisions were made concerning the maintenance of homes and acquisition of equipment items. Residents normally informed a member of visiting support staff of a problem who then contacted the Departmental Buildings Officer. At GH3, however, residents contacted the Local Authority Housing Department directly without the aid of outside support. The Buildings Officer usually made initial equipment inventories for the homes, sometimes with the assistance of the Area Home Help Organiser. Subsequently staff requested items from the Buildings Officer who either provided them directly or else authorised support staff to purchase them. At GH3 the local hospital had been involved in the initial equipping of the home and at GH5 decisions concerning equipment had initially been made by a team of staff and following that through the group home meeting.

In some cases residents suggested to support staff that particular items were needed or repairs needed to be done, in others support staff initiated requisitions themselves. Either way there were limits imposed on what could be done as these matters were considered the responsibility of a separate section of the Social Services Department that dealt with maintenance and equipment in all residential establishments. There was considerable criticism made by staff of the effectiveness of these procedures. Interestingly in most cases a staff member's satisfaction with the procedures related to his position in the hierarchy — that is to say the higher up the hierarchy the more a staff member was satisfied with the procedures in force.

'It's not effective. For example, private drawers and cupboards with locks. I've been pestering him for locks. He's obtained the locks. We're now waiting for him to fix them on. It's been twelve to eighteen months since. In fact I've been pestering him since the group home opened.' (Social Work Assistant)

'Take the toilet bowl and decorations, it's disgusting. It's ages before they get things done and when they do it's often wrong or not what they want.' (Home Help)

In contrast all Area Officers believed that the procedure worked well and that they knew of none of these particular problems.

(vii) *Moving residents out of the home*

There was a high consensus of opinion among staff that a resident would be removed from a group home if he exhibited extreme disruptive behaviour, or if his physical or mental condition rendered it impracticable to remain with the limited support services available. A resident might be considered for transfer to more independent living if he showed a proven ability to survive. Several staff, however, considered that it was their first task to enable residents to survive permanently as a group, indicating either that they did not think it appropriate to move residents on to more independent living or that they were unclear as to what was the overall official policy. Decisions to remove a resident from a home had been reached following the occurrence of a series of incidents and joint consultations among members of the support team, although ultimate decisions had been made by senior members of the support team and had sometimes involved the Medical Consultant.

In particular cases, it was clear that staff considered it unrealistic to move residents on to more independent living owing to their age or to the fact that they were already managing quite well as a group. They had encouraged residents to function interdependently and make allowances for each other such that in their view, it might be proving harmful to individuals to move them on. On the other hand, there were particular residents whom it was thought should be given an opportunity to live by themselves because they did not mix well in the group or because they had expressed a wish to live alone or with one other person.

The files relating to GH1, 2 and 5 described the problems caused in each case by one resident that had led eventually to her removal from the home. The information illustrated the means used by respective support teams in dealing with a 'crisis' situation, how difficult residents had been managed and how, in each case, the end result had been to remove the person out to alternative accommodation (two to hospital, one to a hostel). Two particular factors had emerged as being significant: firstly that the decision to remove a resident from a home had been taken following a series of incidents over a period of time rather than as a result of one given incident, and secondly that it had taken place with the approval of all other residents and staff involved.

Repeated stealing of articles from the home, from other residents and from local shops had been a prime cause leading to the dismissal of Wendy (GH1) and Alice (GH5). Other things contributed such as not getting on with the others, being generally disruptive, aggressive or causing emotional chaos between other individuals. In both above cases the initial 'problem', however, sprang from reported theft incidents.

For the case of Wendy, the Social Work Assistant's 'diary' had recorded in it the following:

'July 24th   Visit. Mrs. S. (Home Help) informed me that £5 had been taken from the housekeeping money. Chief suspect seems to be Wendy. Arranged to see the girls on Friday. Discussed the matter with (Principal Social Worker) before visiting again and it was agreed the only thing I could do was warn each girl in turn.
July 25th   Spoke to each girl about the missing money. The only one to protest her innocence was Wendy. The others just listened in silence.'

Much later on further incidents of theft had been recorded:

'24.4.76   Phone call from Manager of Co-op (at Fulwood) to say that he had caught Wendy stealing. Mr. Green said that this was not the first time. He said that at Xmas a pair of slippers had been seen to be taken by Wendy and that he had gone to (GH1) and warned her that if it happened again he would report her to the police. The second time Wendy had taken a large block of chocolate from a stand near the door and Mr. Green had seen her do so. He didn't want to prosecute but felt that he couldn't let the second incident pass. I informed (Principal Social Worker) of the matter and he arranged to go and see Mr. Green the following day.
29.4.76   Wendy came to the Department and confessed about the chocolate but said at first that she hadn't taken the slippers. She insinuated that the culprit was Brenda (Marston). However (Principal Social Worker) saw Wendy and eventually got the truth that she was responsible for both thefts. (Principal Social Worker) saw Mr. Green who said he was prepared to leave the matter with him to deal with.'

The business of dealing with Alice at GH5 had, in contrast, been conducted over a much shorter time period (three months approximately). Thefts had been reported time and time again, and on confrontation, she had broken down in tears. At least following the initial string of incidents, other residents and the Home Helps had continually requested that the losses be overlooked and Alice be forgiven.

'Everyone concerned expressed their desire for Alice to continue living at (GH5) and not for her to be returned to Ward 30 which Alice also tearfully insisted she didn't want to do.'

The Principal Social Worker had discussed these incidents with the hospital staff and discovered 'the surprising information that Alice had an incredibly long history of similar behaviour towards other patients and staff, not only in actual cash but also in personal possessions and even hospital supplies'. Having then had the matter brought up for consideration by the Medical Consultant, the Principal Social Worker was recommended to 'take positive measures now or else the whole future of

(GH5) could be jeopardised because of the present unhappy atmosphere of suspicion'. The Consultant offered to 'swap' Alice for another hospital resident; thus with the agreement of other staff and residents (who had come to accept that Alice was not going to improve) the Principal Social Worker took the decision to have her removed.

Wendy (GH1) had been granted a much longer 'trial' period in the group home despite her recurring thieving and the additional harmful effects of her behaviour on other residents. She had always insisted on having her own way with the others who had sometimes complained but, each time, had been asked to show more tolerance towards her. Jobs had been obtained for her but she had left them on the merest excuse; she had invented stories about other people which had led to a lot of unnecessary work on the part of the Social Work Assistant.

After a year and a half, the Social Work Assistant had decided to seek advice from her senior in the hope that some kind of direct action could have been taken. Her 'diary' had reported 'the final straw':

'18.10.76   Phone call from Wendy's sister to say that Wendy was in the Royal Infirmary after taking an overdose of tablets! I went up to (GH1) and was given a note by Doris which Wendy had left on the table for me. It said that if she couldn't live with Mrs. A. (a Home Help) or her father then her life was over! I phoned the hospital and was told that she was alright and would probably be discharged in a couple of days after seeing a psychiatrist. Wendy's sister came to the Department and we had a discussion about Wendy's action. Her sister said that Wendy had always been dramatic and that she hoped that this incident would not mean she would have to leave (GH1). Apparently Wendy had taken several of the tablets which were prescribed for her kidney trouble but after taking them she had got frightened and had gone out to the telephone kiosk and phoned the hospital. She was seen by the psychiatrist and discharged on Oct. 21st......'

'......(all the other residents) requested that Wendy should be removed. I informed (the Principal Social Worker) of all this and after frequent discussions between him and the Area Officer, it was agreed that Wendy would have to be withdrawn from (GH1).'

The problem of Susan (GH2) had differed in one way from the others in that she had managed successfully to settle in the home for almost three years before her behaviour had begun to deteriorate seriously. Incidents of temper tantrums had been reported and the 'diary' had related 'emergency' incidents whereupon the Social Work Assistant had been requested to intervene either by one of the Home Helps or the residents.

'Arrived at (GH2) during an episode of further trouble. The youngsters were on holiday from the training centre and were upstairs. Violet and Doris were sick and John and Mrs. Ho. (Home Help) were in the process of cleaning up. It was apparent that Susan was the culprit as usual. Seemingly Violet and Doris were getting the washing ready when they found all the drawers full of dirty toilet paper and sanitary towels. The final straw was when Doris put Susan's dressing gown into the washing machine and found the washing machine blocked due to dirty toilet paper, whch came from the pockets. All the girls were very upset and

131

even Mrs. Ho. who tends to play situations down was showing signs of temper and admitted to telling Susan off, as a result of this she had had a further tantrum and thrown herself on the floor. I spoke to Susan myself but she chose to look in the opposite direction and didn't listen to me. When she walked away she muttered things to herself. On returning to the office I reported the matter to (the Specialist Social Worker) who contacted (the Medical Consultant) who thought it necessary for a bed to be found for her to have her observed.'

This had been 'the end' for Susan whose removal had not been disputed by other residents — apart perhaps from Beryl who had been her companion — as in fact they had been in favour of this action for quite a while.

(viii) *Legal status*

Three acts specify the powers and duties of local authorities to provide special residential accommodation for mentally handicapped adults. They are the 1948 National Assistance Act, the 1959 Mental Health Act and the 1968 Health Services and Public Health Act. In the first of these, Part III, Section 21, Cl. 1 declares that,

'It shall be the duty of every local authority to provide residential accommodation for persons who by reason of age, infirmity or any other circumstances are in need of care and attention which is not otherwise available to them. . . . . .'

With regard to the type of care provision to be made available, none of the above legislation is specific although it is stated that it should be 'appropriate to needs'. As for the official legal status of people being cared for under this legislation, arrangements are made on a voluntary basis with no formal restrictions being imposed on the freedom of individual clients. These arrangements applied, with the exception of those in GH3, to the residents of all the present group homes. Since moving to the home the residents in GH3 had officially been classed as 'on extended leave' from the local hospital and hence technically remained as hospital residents.

In relation to the formal status of the buildings being used as group homes, most staff were able to describe additional physical provisions that had been made to the buildings in order that they met with certain official requirements, but further necessary information on the statutory framework governing their formal status had to come from the Buildings Officer. A part of the relevant local authority building regulations concerned with the use of private and rented property where some degree of care or support is provided deals specifically with fire precautions; it designates different kinds of buildings according to their use, in order to define fire hazards and appropriate preventive measures. Among the designated purpose-groups are:

I   Small residential (including ordinary domestic housing)
II Institutional
III Other residential

As a rule, self-contained dwellings including group flatlet schemes with warden supervision, provided under housing powers, are either group I or III. All buildings registered under Part III of the National Assistance Act 1948 are automatically group II. Purpose-group II covers all institutional buildings housing sleeping provision and which cater for the treatment, care or maintenance of elderly or disabled people. It includes hospitals, residential homes, residential schools and holiday accommodation specifically designed to cater for disabled people. It was reported that the normal procedure whereby a social services department acquires an ordinary house from the housing department for care purposes was for it to be designated as purpose-group II. This required an application for planning permission for a 'change of use' which entailed public notification and consultation, and secondly needed to satisfy a set of fire regulations which did not apply to ordinary family homes. These included the installation of fire-fighting equipment, fireproof doors, walls and spaces, alarm systems and emergency exit requirements.

However, the administrative lines between purpose-group I and III and purpose-group II are fine ones. It was reported that considerable discretion in determining the purpose-groups was exercised by officials at local level. In relation to the present houses, discretionary powers prevailed such that no firm rulings were made. For GH1, 2 and 6 minimum conditions were met in the form of additional equipment such as a fire extinguisher, a fireproof door and alarm system. GH5, being sited on hospital grounds contained 'normal hospital fire equipment' which consisted of the above items plus a smoke detector and emergency lighting. Neither GH3 nor GH4 contained fire equipment. The Buildings Officer stated that he had had no involvement with GH3, whereas GH4 had been treated by the local fire officer as a 'normal residence'. GH4 was the most recent home to come into operation: 'When we got (GH4) I asked them about the arrangements. They said, "Oh, we'll treat it as a normal residence with a maximum of five residents allowed" and so no fire equipment was needed'. (Buildings Officer)

(ix) *Staff objectives*

A wide range of terms were employed by staff in describing the people they were serving, including 'high grade mentally handicapped' and 'subnormals who don't need much support'. Other terms included 'inadequates', 'backward', 'people who are a bit slow' and people who are 'feebleminded', 'institutionalised' or simply 'elderly'. Descriptions did not emphasise the degree of handicap or indicate, in the main, that people were severely handicapped so as to render them inappropriate for a

133

group home. Several Home Helps, in particular, de-emphasised mental handicap in making descriptions, 'they're not ordinary like you or I really — they're nervous types. They can get a bit bewildered sometimes. They're nice and pleasant though', or 'people who've had a bad start in life with their families'.

In general, aims for the homes were described either as 'to make residents live as independently as possible', or 'to help them to live a normal life'. Other aims were also referred to — 'to create a home, to improve (residents') quality of life, to increase their happiness'. Some staff showed that they were unclear as to the aims of the home; one Home Help expressed disillusionment — 'We're doing nothing really; we're taking them out of their environment where they're happy. They're happier in institutions than being brought out. They can't communicate with people and people can't with them.' Staff referred to a number of ways and means used by them for achieving their goals; these included building up residents' confidence, encouraging them to take their own decisions, encouraging them to do 'normal things' such as using community facilities, teaching them tasks and encouraging their independence ('to function as a family'). Home Helps emphasised the teaching of domestic skills.

Many staff, particularly those from GH2, 5 and 6, believed that different types of resident were more suited to their homes — 'those with more potential', 'the younger age group', 'people from family backgrounds'. Had they had a preferred group, they stated that they would have introduced more 'training programmes', used multidisciplinary assessments, individual programme plans, monitoring and done more outside liaison work. These were examples of things individual staff said they would do in a new set of circumstances. Asked for their views on whether they considered that the home should be 'their permanent residence', attitudes differed widely, although there was high agreement at GH2 and 3 that the arrangement should be permanent. Others said that particular residents should be allowed to move on and several expressed the general view that it was for the residents to decide. Factors such as age differences and the need for separate two-person accommodation required a flexible approach.

Staff gave their views on the sorts of mentally handicapped people they considered suitable for living in group homes. The question was limited insofar as answers were based on personal definitions of a group home. Opinions expressed, for example, by GH1 respondents, varied although presenting a pattern of Social Work staff perceiving a flexible use of group homes and Home Helps perceiving them in more prescriptive terms.

Area Officer

'We should be prepared to experiment and extend (them) to the more dependent, because we can always move them back if we find they're not capable...... '

Principal Social Worker

'Any group of individuals who are compatible for group living. IQ is less important.'

Home Helps

'(Those) who are continent, ambulant, capable of personal self-care', and '(Those) who had jobs or else had a chance of getting a job.'

Social Work staff associated with GH2 perceived group homes as being only appropriate for people with relatively high levels of intelligence and independent functioning, although Home Helps perceived them for a wider mix of people.

Home Helps

'Age and personality mix are important. You can't have someone who is really backward or handicapped because they're going to have to carry that one person', and '(exclude) violent and physically handicapped people, all the rest could manage.'

Most staff from GH3 stated that a resident's ability to learn 'social skills' was the primary criterion; the 'difficulty with physically handicapped people' was also mentioned, as was a willingness to 'take anyone provided they don't need continuous support'. The person in closest contact with the home, the Nursing Assistant, mentioned 'those (mentally handicapped) people with favourable personalities, those who are willing to learn'. At GH4 there was a view that given current support only 'a restricted number of people' would be eligible though naturally this would change if 'more support (was) given'. Individual GH5 staff excluded residents with 'anti-social habits' or 'severe physical handicaps', although the Area Officer was prepared to take a wider view:

'(They should cater for) a wide range of mentally handicapped people, those with potential for independence and those with lower abilities for whom you can only provide a home, provided of course that they were able to live in a group and gell.'

Views expressed by staff from GH6 were again varied: those 'with good personalities', 'who can get on together', 'who aren't aggressive and don't have personality disorders', 'who have no families of their own with whom they could live', 'who have some experience of a hostel-type situation, or have previously been supported by parents' and 'not those with very low IQs'.

One reason why staff laid stress on the above criteria was the limit imposed by available support services. Other reasons were given, for example, at GH1 the Area Officer took the view that more mentally handicapped people should be provided for in group homes both for financial ('It is cheaper than providing residential care in hostels') and social reasons ('The public should be made aware of their responsibilities', 'the mentally handicapped deserve a normal life'). Other staff stressed the importance of the group being 'integrated' and 'fitting into' the local neighbourhood. Selection criteria would depend on the amount and quality of staff support available.

'If residents need higher staffing levels then the object of providing ordinary care in the community is lost as the concept changes. As a result the home becomes distinguished from the rest of the community.' (Principal Social Worker, GH2)

The need for community acceptance, for a stable well-mixed group of residents and the difficulty of providing extra staff support justified the main criteria set by staff. The 'difficulty with physically handicapped people' was stated as being that 'they would not be able to use public transport and to do their own shopping, also they would put too many constraints on other residents'. The premise that the amount of staffing support available to a home was finite imposed a restriction on the types of 'individual' resident whom it was thought could be managed.

'Those who need a lot of support require resident staff. The idea of a group home is that it functions without staff for most of the time'. (Principal Social Worker, GH5)

Finally, there was the question of in-service training for staff — the position throughout was rather negative. Admittedly, several Home Helps had attended a short (usually one week) course, but judging from their responses it had little relevance to the job they were faced with. 'It was no use really, you didn't learn anything. You weren't talking about specific people who came from these homes......' Several staff, both Social Work and Home Help, commented on how training would have been useful though no opinions were sought on the type needed.

(x) *Summary*

The arrangements and procedures relating to each home differed quite markedly. For the majority of administrative purposes the homes were Area-based and this decentralisation was reflected in the heterogeneous pattern of arrangements that had evolved. The main similarities among homes concerned their use of centralised resources, for example, the Departmental Buildings Section, in matters relating to their maintenance, equipment and legal classification and the Assessment Section, in matters relating to the management of residents' finances. In the majority of cases, there was an overall lack of clear official policy for the homes reflected in, for example, an absence of goal setting, staff procedures, relevant staff training, admission criteria and decision-making arrangements. There was evidence of internal confusion regarding the roles of staff particularly at the direct-care level and regarding the lines of accountability within each administrative structure.

There were, however, examples of a more structural approach exemplified in the selection and decision-making arrangements of particular homes yet at the same time there was no evidence to show that these practices had been brought to bear elsewhere or at least that experience had been shared or communicated among homes within the Department. The role of each respective Area Officer as an overall administrator had been emphasised and likewise, the extent to which some individuals provided a coordinating function within a support team, yet it was also the case that knowledge and views varied among staff within a home in relation to set issues. Often the range of views corresponded to the staff hierarchical structure so as to suggest that official position was related to perception and knowledge of a given issue. There were some areas of conformity of approach among homes, for example, in procedures for introducing new residents and the circumstances relating to their removal, as there were areas in which there was a high consensus of staff opinion, for example, on goals for the homes, desirable treatment methods, the nature of appropriate residents, the need to provide social and recreational activities and the effectiveness of procedures to obtain repairs and equipment.

Whereas internal decision-making and the monitoring of procedures had not been undertaken formally, there were examples of informal and ad-hoc methods appertaining to individual homes, that had consisted of one-to-one decision-making and monitoring carried out through already established staff supervision arrangements. Finally, there had been few changes, in the period examined, in the support arrangements provided for each home; the principal one had been the overall minor reduction or change in Home Help support and its consequent implications for the management of residents' affairs, particularly in relation to finance, social and recreational activities and the teaching of domestic skills. Taking this as a criterion, there have been relatively few examples of conscious effort towards achieving greater resident independence.

SECTION 4

Overview

The findings provide strong evidence to support the view that the group homes evolved in a random, ad-hoc way producing confusion and uncertainty among staff at different levels of the official hierarchy. There was some evidence on how policy decisions were made but little on why they were made. In the early days there were differences of opinion between middle and senior management representatives regarding issues such as the financial entitlements of residents and the limitations on staff support. There was a consistent division between the two, highlighting the greater determination of middle management to 'take risks' in the extent to which they were prepared to allow residents to be independent. The lines of accountability between staff were often blurred and this is particularly apparent at the top of the hierarchy. Area Officers experienced a sense of isolation and frustration resulting in no clear directives emerging for respective group homes not least owing to the insufficiency of staffing resources available.

The intervention of different staff at different levels in the solution of problems, for example, financial entitlements or the selection of residents, served to emphasise the confused power structure and system of decision-making. Whereas it could be argued that there were valid reasons for certain individuals to become involved in certain matters, practice indicated that there was a lack of coordination within the Department and an absence of rational decision-making. To take the example of residents' financial entitlements: the local DHSS eventually determined these amounts following receipt of advice from both the Director of Social Services and the Departmental Assessments Officer. Evidence has illustrated how Area Officers dealt with these two officers rather than directly with the DHSS, despite the fact that Area Officers had comparatively closer contact with residents and hence were more aware of their needs. It did not follow that both the Director and the Assessments Officer represented the views and interests of the Area Officers as it became clear that in certain cases these did not coincide. Not only that, but it was also unclear whether there existed an established line of communication between this group of officers for discussion of financial or other matters. What, for example, if any, were the roles of the Assistant Directors or the Principal Assistant (Mental Health)? And why should the Director see fit to intervene on this issue to the exclusion of a whole range of other relevant issues, potentially of equal or greater importance?

The Department contained no one officer or group of officers with a particular over-riding responsibility for group homes which is a factor posing difficulties in relation to the effectiveness of inter-agency cooperation. Despite the proof of a limited co-operation between the different agencies, evidence showed that no established channels existed and that the results of ad-hoc liaison depended on individual circumstances. There was evidence of strong feelings being shown by certain Area Officers towards senior management, that took the form of written requests proposing that the latter take an 'upper hand' in setting out policy. It is at this level within the organisation that the need for policy-making was paramount.

The Area Officers were effectively placed 'in charge' of their respective homes but without support from the tiers of the hierarchy placed above. The heterogeneous development of group homes without management support occurred within the limits of resources available to each Area, hence limiting the extent to which each Area could properly set planning targets. Thus although an Area Officer might be placed in overall charge, he could not compel a Home Help Organiser or Principal Social Worker to 'take on' a group home without, at the same time, accepting the need for a 'shift' in the total resources available. This may account in some way for unintended developments occurring in group homes, because Area Officers, by force of circumstance, had to leave their teams to organise support for the homes without the official monitoring they would normally consider desirable. Granted the experimental nature of group homes and the limits of staffing resources, it is still never clear what *type* of staff the authorities thought it desirable to use. A combination of Social Work and Home Help support presented problems in administrative accountability, but there is also the problem of matching the required task to the staff resources available and accepting the inevitable need for the adaptation of staff roles.

The findings have shown the difficulties that arose from placing Home Helps in the group homes. One of the chief points concerned the extent to which Home Helps functioned as 'teachers' to residents in encouraging their independence. To take the example of GH2 and 5 as they happened to be the group homes receiving permanent Home Help support: in both cases there was conflict between Social Work and Home Help staff regarding the role of the latter. Social Work staff had argued that Home Helps were too overprotective; if this was true then the effect might appear in residents' assessment scores as individual residents would be expected to make less than average gains, particularly on Personal Independence. However, whereas the mean number of domains in which an individual improved overall was 9.5, GH2 residents improved on 14, 23, 15, 11 and 15 domains and GH5 on 13 and 8 respectively, suggesting an *above average* level of overall improvement. This shows that group homes with the higher support staff-resident ratio made greater gains than those with a lower ratio.

It is difficult to analyse properly the effects the Home Helps had on the residents. Again taking the case of GH2: Mrs. He. was disliked by at least some of the residents, probably because her attitude to them was both overbearing and overprotective, and they had little real opportunity to learn new skills yet, according to the ABS score, improvement within this home was the most impressive. From available evidence, it is not possible to reconcile these apparently conflicting factors, although several points are worth noting, for example: Beryl was 'mothered' not only by Mrs. He. but also by the other female residents; the limited number of household jobs available to residents meant that the females would squabble over them arguing that one was more able than the other to carry

139

them out; John was seen by the other residents (including his wife) as a placid leader figure; Doris Grantham's occasional outbursts of aggressive behaviour led the others to 'rally round' and consider how to deal with the problem. These were the main themes running through relationships of residents which might explain some of the change that occurred.

The whole 'caring' approach used by the Home Helps deserves consideration. To what extent did they over-react to the situations facing them and over-identify with the residents, rather than try to develop and maintain a 'professional' detachment from them? Some definitions of clients given by Home Helps do not recognise that the former are mentally handicapped.

The close daily contact the Home Helps had with residents might account for this, as their attitudes towards them may have changed. Most Home Helps aimed to be friendly to residents and their friendships may have prevented them from being able to assess needs more objectively. GH1 Home Helps' resentment of being withdrawn was related to the close friendships they had developed with the residents (although there was no evidence to suggest that residents behaved in an unfriendly way to the Social Work Assistant who took over).

This is one of the issues relating to the deployment of untrained staff in group homes. It is not to suggest directly that they are unsuitable but that it is likely to be more difficult to gain their cooperation in a treatment programme for a resident if they are not aware of some of the underlying reasons for implementing it. If these can be explained satisfactorily with or without the experience of training, then the result might be acceptable; however, the above findings suggest that the experience of using untrained staff had negative effects such as to possibly outweigh any direct advantages gained.

There is also the administrative and organisational side to the Home Help issue: is it reasonable to expect them to succeed on their own? Home Helps are traditionally accustomed to serving other client groups, notably the elderly and in each of the present cases, working in a group home for the mentally handicapped was a new experience for them. For many Home Helps this may have been preferable as the work appeared 'lighter'. However, the data show that Home Helps were initially appointed on a voluntary basis as the job involved 'anti-social' hours. This being the case, Home Help Organisers felt a commitment to ensuring their Home Helps some degree of job security and hence, as the case of GH5 illustrated, an Organiser's unwillingness to actively support Social Workers in the achievement of their goals of promoting independence was related to her priority of protecting the interests of her staff.

This underlines the need for a teamwork approach in providing support to group homes, that involves Home Helps and Social Workers working closely together, following an objective appraisal of the overall needs of residents. The experience, for example, of a Principal Social Worker requesting the withdrawal of Home Helps via the Home Help Organiser without directly contacting and explaining the situation to the Home Helps themselves led to resentment by Home Helps towards the Social Workers (Section B ii.). At GH5 the Principal Social Worker admitted that Organisers had made a 'wrong choice' of Home Helps — 'For quite unknown reasons they have retarded the residents' progress and seriously delayed our projected treatment goals' (Section B ii.). This illustrated the poor communication between staff, as 'our' treatment goals implied that they were exclusive to Social Workers. It emphasised the need to spell out goals for the home and determine in a practical way how they might be applied. The Social Workers found it extremely difficult to have an established Home Help removed and were forced to tolerate an unacceptable state of affairs until the Area Officer had to be called in to reassess the situation.

GH2 and 5 were the only group homes that held regular staff meetings but the evidence has shown that both, in spite of this, had serious staff problems concerned with the definition of individual roles and staff accountability. GH2 meetings dealt with day-to-day problems concerning residents' activities, whereas GH5 meetings usually tried to tackle the more serious issues concerning the abilities of residents and their need for outside support. The existence of staff meetings in neither case appeared fruitful in solving the major staff problems that have been alluded to in this chapter. GH2 meetings hardly touched on the 'real issues' that rankled, for example, the role of Home Helps, and they lacked the authority to bring about any major staff changes. This lack of authority applied equally to GH5's meetings, although it must be said that the Principal Social Worker became gradually accredited with the role of Area representative, having authority delegated directly by the Area Officer. Another factor was that Social Workers were outnumbered in these meetings by Home Helps in the ratio 1:2, lessening any opportunity the former had to challenge the latter's position.

The data have referred to 'link-men' existing in relation to particular homes, notably GH1 and GH6. The importance of having one main coordinating person responsible for a home should be emphasised, particularly when no staff meetings are organised for the purpose of enabling communication among staff. The 'link-man' for GH1 was, however, the Principal Social Worker who was not 'home-based' which proved to have some negative consequences for relationships between staff and residents at the home level.

Excluding GH2 and 5 staff meetings, the only other references to staff convening to discuss a group home were those concerned with the initial selection of residents and the setting up of a home. The findings referred to meetings attended by a range of relatively senior officers from within the Department such as the Assessments Officer, the Principal Assistant (Mental Health) and Area Officers. Each of these people brought to bear their own criteria and terms of reference in making decisions on what was advisable and largely the result reflected their views, position and the resources currently available to them. As regards the actual criteria for selecting residents, these were not explicit from the data. However, one thing is certain, and that is that choices were made primarily by the Medical Consultant — in only one case, GH4, was it clear that only Social Work staff were involved. It then appeared as policy that once the homes had been set up, initial groups selected and social work intervention established, all subsequent selections would be made by Social Workers.

The details of initial selection policies were hence largely unclear although in the case of GH3 and 4 there had been an initial pre-selection followed by a strategy of observing the effects of individuals interrelating spontaneously as a group in order to pick out suitable ones for 'trial' in the home. GH3 residents were selected following experience in a domestic training unit (a house in the hospital grounds) though there was no evidence to show that there had ever been consideration to use this facility more widely. Following various incidents of individuals from the originally selected groups proving to be unsatisfactory residents the Medical Consultant had continued to be involved through her selection of additional residents then currently in hospital whom she agreed to 'swap' for a resident in the group home. This continued involvement was related to the fact that the Social Worker attached to the home wanted a hospital place for the 'problem' resident and it was only via the Consultant that this could be obtained.

CHAPTER 5

Summary and Conclusions

The introduction to the research on page 25 set out the aims of this study and the particular hypotheses to be tested. It is now approriate to refer back and summarise the *main findings* taking the study as a whole.

SECTION 1

Original Hypotheses

(i) *Group home residents were more able than LA hostel residents in Personal Independence skills* (Part I of the ABS)

On all but one of the domains on Part I of the A–B Scale, group home scores were higher, with significant differences shown on domains headed Economic Activity, Language Development, Numbers and Time and Domestic Activity. It was not possible to show that these same differences were apparent at the time residents were moved into the group homes so as to suggest that they constituted admission criteria. It may have been that such 'self-help' skills were more easily acquired in a group home than a hostel. It is important to add that a similarly low level of 'maladaptive behaviour' was found among the residents of both LA group homes and hostels. Behaviour factors were found to be the main reason for individual 'failure' in a group home and hence it deserves to be noted that the overall amount of 'maladaptive behaviour' contained within the group homes was broadly similar to that found in the sample of LA hostel residents.

(ii) *Residents in group homes having a high support staff–resident ratio showed greater gains on the A–B Scale than those with less favourable support staff–resident ratios*

GH2 and 5, unlike the other homes, received permanent Home Help support in addition to that from Social Work staff. Out of a maximum 24 domains on the ABS, the five residents from GH2 made gains on 14, 23, 15, 11 and 15 domains and the two from GH5 on 13 and 8 domains. Given that the mean number of domains where an individual made gains, taking the group home population as a whole, was 9.5, those from GH2 and 5 made an above average number of gains.

143

(iii) *Group behaviour factors affected the success/failure of the group homes*

Firstly, it is important to set out the criteria to be used in determining 'success' and 'failure'. Main aims stated by staff were 'independence' and 'normalisation' and any attempt to evaluate success/failure using these aims as a measure should relate to the general criteria they impose. The evidence has illustrated the positive contribution made by group behaviour to resident problem-solving, the practicalities of day-to-day living arrangements, individual skill learning and improving residents' quality of life in general. An examination of the interpersonal relationships among residents showed the existence of role-taking, scapegoating, mothering, sub-groups, leader-follower relationships and others. These data have also shown that individual resident 'failure' in a home largely resulted from disruptive behaviour which led to an individual being rejected by the other residents.

Group interaction contributed to the ability of the groups to survive intact and when individuals had to be removed from a home, this had been due to their recurring disruptive behaviour which had led to a consensus of opposition on the part of other residents and staff. The 'successes' in terms of individual skill learning on Part I of the A−B Scale (Personal Independence) cannot directly be attributed to group interaction factors, although there is evidence to show that these played a decisive part. High overall gains had occurred (on Personal Independence domains) at GH2 and 3, and in each of the larger homes, GH1, 2 and 3 there had been overall gains in group skill-related domains — Self-direction, Responsibility and Socialisation.

The first major section of this study has described and analysed the characteristics of group interaction referring to both their cohesive and divisive qualities, but all of these had in common the fact that they contributed to the dynamics and survival of a group. The role-taking and rota system for sharing household tasks showed that residents devised their own independent means for coping rather than having to rely on outside support. The 'leader/follower' and 'mothering' relationships showed how the more able could assist the less able again with the result of lessening the need for outside support. These were examples of group interaction that had positive implications for increasing the independence and self-respect of individual residents. The relative 'independence' of the group homes (from staff intervention) allowed relationships among residents to develop freely and spontaneously whilst also placing an emphasis on the need for residents to take some degree of initiative in organising their daily living arrangements.

The 'give and take' aspect of personal relationships can be a powerful binding quality resulting in individuals learning to live dependent on each other rather than apart. This growth of interdependence is enriching for the individual as it requires an active contribution from him. The development of individual and group identity has been clear in a number of cases — take the example of Gladys and Bertha (GH3) for instance. These two took the roles of 'group leader' and 'cook' respectively, earning them recognition in the eyes of other group members (and staff) and boosting their personal morale. Ruth's close friendship with Shirley (GH4) helped to improve the former's confidence, and from being shy and extremely withdrawn on entering the home she gradually appeared more relaxed and sociable. There were further examples of individuals 'coming out' and developing on a personal level as this was a relatively common factor associated with all the homes.

(iv) *Group home residents received their main outside support from official sources rather than from informal ones*

Without the intervention of representatives from the official support agency, unofficial support, for example, through friends, neighbours and relatives, was very limited. Even at this level, group homes varied in the amount of informal contacts they received as did the individuals within each of the homes.

Contacts with relatives were usually through a resident visiting a relative's home rather than vice versa. As for neighbourhood contact, the majority of residents stated that they knew at least one next-door neighbour, that conversation with neighbours was brief, usually consisting of no more than a simple address, and that, in general, it was initiated more by neighbours than the residents. The fact of having a next-door neighbour who was also employed officially as a Home Help was important in terms of providing reliable and permanent support and of extending the range of informal contacts available to residents. There were hardly any examples of residents having friends from within the local neighbourhood, as most named friends were work colleagues, co-residents, or mentally handicapped people from another residential unit. The main type of support residents received from official agencies was that of advice in problem-solving, the resolution of internal disputes and other practical matters, such as the management of finances.

SECTION 2

Additional Findings

(i) *Previous residential placement did not influence successful group home placement*

A high proportion of the residents had experienced long-term hospitalisation but this was not related to their success in living in a group home.

Of the eleven residents whose abilities had improved on ten or more domains of the ABS, nine had spent ten or more years in hospital. The other two had been in either hospital or hostel but for a shorter period, approximately four and five years respectively. The only group home (GH4) where all the residents had *not* spent time in hospital showed an overall deterioration in their abilities. Those who had 'failed' had varied backgrounds. The files contained a number of past professional judgements made on group home residents which wrongly predicted their inability to survive in a community setting.

(ii) *The abilities and behaviours of the group home residents had either improved, deteriorated or remained the same according to the two-year follow-up assessment on the A-B Scale*

There was a marked overall 'improvement' in one home (GH2), a marked overall 'deterioration' in another (GH4) and a marked overall 'no change' in a further one (GH1). It has been suggested that improvements in abilities and behaviour were related, among other things, to higher staffing support, staff teaching and group interaction.

(iii) *The Social Services Department (Department of Family and Community Services) had no clear policy for the organisation and administration of its group homes*

The lack of policy led to ineffective operational arrangements at management and direct care level. Area Officers were unsure as to how their group homes should operate and ended up making independent arrangements within existing staff resources available to them. There had been disagreements between middle (Area Officers) and higher management (Assistant Director upwards) over the extent to which residents should be allowed to cope independently, that had usually been resolved in favour of the former. There had been interdepartmental cooperation in the setting up of two homes that had involved joint action between Social Services (F and CS) and the Area Health Authority.

Serious problems had arisen in relation to the role of definition of Home Helps who had been providing support to residents in the homes. There had been argument and confusion over the nature of their tasks and their accountability to management. Their relationship with the Social Workers had at best been based on a tolerant acceptance of one another and at worst had created stressful conditions, all largely owing to the refusal of management to take an 'upper hand' in the situation. Some Home Helps had expressed reservation on their being qualified to do this kind of work, whereas others had insisted on being over-involved in the lives of the residents to a degree that conflicted with the usually more clear stated aims of Social Workers to encourage residents to live independently.

The similarities in the administrative arrangements of homes occurred in their use of the Department's centralised resources, for example, the Buildings Section (equipment, maintenance, legal classification) and the Assessments Section (residents' finances, payment of bills). Otherwise the heterogeneous development of group homes arose as a result of independent Area-based initiatives without the overriding support of management. The lack of policy was most clearly seen in the absence of goal setting, staff procedures, admission criteria and decision-making arrangements. Where there had been evidence of the use of a more structured approach in, for example, selection methods and decision-making, these had been isolated cases as communication was in general lacking between the teams of support staff for the group homes which restricted the extent to which 'good practice' could be transmitted around the Department.

(iv) *The criteria used for the selection of residents for group homes had been implicit rather than explicit, and in general, were not clear at all*

In the majority of cases the Medical Consultant, with or without the assistance of nursing staff, had made initial selections based on criteria which were largely implicit from her written reports and assessments. Recommendations stressed the importance of social competence and personality traits, in particular, basic self-care, the ability to perform simple domestic work and work aptitude. Reference had also been made to original 'misplacement' *i.e.* where a resident never ought to have been in hospital in the first place, hence implying that he/she was an obvious candidate for 'the community'. There had been use made of a 'group dynamics' approach in selection though it had not been clear upon what basis the original larger groups had been selected (a number of 'possibles' had first been selected and then observed by staff over a period of time to see how well they interacted as a group and how well they were capable of undertaking a series of tasks).

SECTION 3

Implications of Findings

Having presented the main findings, it is appropriate to consider some of their implications and to make suggestions for future service provision. The present emphasis in government policy has been on the need to provide residential care that is homelike, locally-based and small in scale. There has been a lack of central and local government commitment towards developing community options and resolving the fundamental problem of the need to match care and support to the individual needs of residents. Very little research evidence has been found concerning the viability of small community units, other than that which suggests that small living units are generally associated with a high quality of resident care. What lessons can be drawn from the present research findings for determining future policy towards group home care?

The importance of grouping

Mentally handicapped adults from a wide range of residential backgrounds can be suited to live in a group home. It is important to obtain the 'right grouping' of individuals in terms of skills and personalities in order that the group can live together satisfactorily and be able to benefit, such as learning new skills and improving the behaviour of individual residents. Taking the present research findings, the amount of individual 'maladaptive' behaviour found amongst the sample of hostel residents was shown to be broadly similar to that of the group home residents, suggesting that individuals possessing behaviour problems can be managed within a group home.

Group homes can therefore offer a residential care option to a wide range of mentally handicapped adults. There are no clear-cut criteria on who should or should not be admissible for residence as, in theoretical terms, all types of mentally handicapped people are able to live in group homes given the necessary support. The essential point is that individuals should be combined in a manner that enables them to share their skills and attributes. The emphasis needs to be on encouraging interdependence among a group of people, on enabling the more able to aid the less able and on treating individuals as people with attributes that can harmonise with those of others in a beneficial way. No matter how mentally and physically capable a person is, he needs others around him to function effectively. Living in a group home and having close daily contact with other residents can help an individual to socialise and establish a personal identity which can then help him to freely develop social relationships outside of the home.

The need for flexibility in staff deployment

The main types of support provided to residents were in the form of *doing* practical tasks and *solving* individual and group problems. Different staff were associated with different tasks — Home Helps undertook practical and domestic tasks and sometimes these involved teaching residents, whilst Social Workers solved problems, managed certain areas of residents' lives and taught specific skills. The resultant confusion over relative responsibilities indicates that clearer definition is required of the needs of a group of residents and for these to be matched with whatever support staff should work together as a team with aims that are both precise and practicable and with their responsibilities clearly marked out. Flexibility is demanded in a situation where aims are changing constantly and good working partnerships are needed both to specify aims clearly and to decide on methods of work.

The need to identify and organise community resources

Simply placing mentally handicapped adults to live in ordinary houses in a community does not ensure that they will develop contacts there. This study has shown that most informal contacts depended on the intervention of official support workers. A next-door neighbour employed as a Home Help proved extremely effective in providing 'on-tap' support, giving information to other support workers and in establishing resident contact with neighbours in the local vicinity. If residents are to fit into a neighbourhood then support workers should find out about facilities offered, make contacts with neighbours and inform them in a sensitive way about the residents, and, most of all, encourage the residents themselves to socialise with local people. A similar sort of official intervention is needed with residents' relatives, for the findings showed how, despite lengthy periods spent in hospital, certain residents still continued to make contact with particular relatives, usually siblings. Although it might not be possible to extend these contacts, it would be useful to reappraise them in the light of a resident's changed life-style.

The need for clear management policy and guidance

In order to constitute a viable alternative type of residential provision, group homes need effective administrative back-up and support. Primarily, a clear statement of aims is needed backed-up by Departmental approval and funding. For example, admission criteria are needed that relate to and correspond with operational criteria used for other types of residential care available. Staff tasks need to be outlined and questions of accountability resolved, including the role of Social Services Department 'specialists' such as the Assessments and Building Section, Principal Assistants and Specialist Social Workers. If group homes are to operate at an Area level then adequate links with fieldwork teams and domiciliary services need to be formed. The main difficulty in administrative terms concerns deciding on the appropriate type of staff structure and administration for group homes and trying to fit this into the existing Departmental organisation. Secondly, the development of group homes necessitates the build up of effective relationships with the external agencies, for instance, the area Health Authority, the DHSS and the Housing Department. These need to be worked out through the aid of officers delegated to act with responsibility for coordination, but who also have sufficient contact with the homes themselves. Overall, a uniform approach is required with Area teams maintaining some degree of collaboration with one another to ensure that good practice is shared, that staff morale is kept high and outcomes for residents are as beneficial as possible.

SECTION 4

Government Reports

The Jay Report*, for example, recommends a model of care based on ordinary housing which includes specialised staffed homes, group homes and accommodation shared with non-handicapped people. Adult residential accommodation 'should meet a continuum of individual need ranging from maximum support and protection to minimal professional involvement in the life of an essentially independent person' (para. 133). Its proposed service model is intended to facilitate rather than hamper the integration of handicapped people into society, and is based on the following principles (para. 93):

(a) Mentally handicapped people should use normal services wherever possible. Special provisions tend to set apart those who receive them and may therefore increase the distance between mentally handicapped people and the rest of society.

(b) Existing networks of community support should be strengthened by professional services rather than supplanted by them.

(c) 'Specialised' services or organisations for mentally handicapped people should be provided only to the extent that they demonstrably meet or are likely to meet additional needs that cannot be met by the general services. Often these specialised services will be required only intermittently or as one component in a more general service. Often the aim will be to provide 'back-up' to a more general service. Wherever possible the special services should be delivered in integrated settings. In the past such services have often been specialised only in name, they have not met defined special needs.

(d) If we are to meet the many and diverse needs of mentally handicapped people we need maximum coordination of services both within and between agencies and at all levels. The concept of a life plan† seems essential if coordination and continuity of care is to be achieved.

(e) Finally, if we are to establish and maintain high quality services for

---

* Report of the Committee of Enquiry into Mental Handicap Nursing and Care. Volumes I and II. Cmnd. 7468. HMSO 1979.
† A 'life plan' means that for every mentally handicapped individual the delivery of services should be mapped out in advance. At any one time the aims of the present care regime and the options which will be open in the future should be known to all those involved.

a group who cannot easily articulate and press their just claims, we need someone to intercede on behalf of mentally handicapped people in obtaining services.

As regards group home provision for adults (paras. 138 and 139), the report firstly supports the notion that group homes should allow a handicapped adult to develop the confidence and the ability to initiate a move beyond supported accommodation into independent living. Secondly, it states, 'For others, placement in an unstaffed but supported group home will represent the maximum kind of independence that they will be able to manage'. The proposals made are as follows:

(1) Group homes should not (only) be an option for the most able. 'Often in a mixed ability group one member is able to complement another in terms of household management of personality.'

(2) Group homes should be open to those who have 'lived in staffed accommodation for many years'.

'(Group homes) can provide an opportunity for the development of skills that have remained latent for decades.'

(3) 'The amount of support that a particular group (home) needs may vary over time and flexibility must be built (in).'

'The first solution to the problem of an individual who is not doing too well should not be to look for an alternative placement in a staffed home. Making homes of this kind work will demand a lot from support staff. Institutional approaches of the kind described by King, Raynes and Tizard (1971) are not confined to institutions. They can emerge in professional practice in the community'.

(4) The provision of a number of group homes should make it possible, where there is incompatibility among the members of one group, for individuals to move to and join another group.

(5) There are advantages in employing as a staff member a person living in close proximity to the group home, especially a next-door neighbour.

'This would allow more regular on-going contact than is likely to be possible from visiting support staff.'

The above proposals take an extremely flexible view of the role of groups homes in terms of the range of mentally handicapped adults able to be contained within them. They do not directly preclude any type of mentally handicapped individual on grounds such as his ability or previous residential experience. The attitude towards the provision of staffing support is an equally flexible one — an acceptance of the need for both formal and informal types of support dependent on the needs of a particular group of residents. There is the expectation that staff should try to resolve individual resident problems arising from within the homes, but an acceptance also of the fact that, where incompatibility is found to exist among individuals, there should be other group homes in which individuals could, with assistance, be placed.

These proposals tie in with findings of this research, which suggest a potential for 'widening the net' of mentally handicapped individuals suitable for group homes. They accept the practicality of admitting people other than 'the most able', mainly on the grounds that individual skill levels alone are less important than what results from the mixing of individual skills and personalities within a group. This argument is given weight by the proposal to 'vary' the type and amount of staffing support depending on the needs of the specific group.

However, the report implicitly places a limit on the level of individual disability capable of being contained within a group home by its alternative proposal for staffed homes with a higher level of support. 'It is clear (para. 141) that many mentally handicapped adults will need considerably more help than could sensibly be offered by the kinds of accommodation we have described above' i.e. Independent Living, para. 137; Group Homes, paras. 138, 139; Accommodation Shared with Non-handicapped People, para. 140. Staffed accommodation using ordinary housing is proposed (paras. 141–143) for this remaining group owing to their demand for 'very intensive' and/or 'highly skilled staffing support'. Thus the real difference between a 'group home' and a 'staffed home' can only be seen in terms of the type and amount of staffing it receives, for example, daily visits as opposed to twenty-four hour care.

The other main proposal of the Jay Report concerning the need for flexible staffing arrangements in group homes is strongly supported by the present findings, which suggest a need to define staff tasks, to match these with available resources and to review both in the light of the residents' changing needs. The Report stresses a need for 'continuity' in individual resident relationships together with a need for 'localness' and 'maximum physical integration' of the homes within the neighbourhood, all of which justify the need for employing neighbours as support staff. The present findings show both the successes attained through the formal use of neighbours for this purpose and suggest the need to build-in to the role of support staff a duty to develop the neighbourhood contacts of individual group home residents.

The Development Team (Third Report (1982)) makes no clear reference to the range of need to be accommodated in group homes but instead relates to the type of support required, placing an emphasis on Home Helps as opposed to professional social work support:

'We have seen successful group homes being sustained by involvement from Home Helps rather than professional social workers. The value to the group of the support from Home Helps was not in actually carrying out tasks but in advising on what needed to be done, and how, in practical aspects of daily living.'

SECTION 5

A Proposed Model of Group Home Provision

The findings suggest a need to define how group homes might be provided as a viable residential care option for mentally handicapped adults. This section attempts to present some of the key elements comprising a service model and to make recommendations for the kind of role that each should play.

(i) *Management and housing*

Given the wide range of administrative needs associated with any expansion of group home provision an agency would be wise to consider the option of appointing officers directly concerned with their development. This section refers to some of the issues involved in the appointment of *group home managers* attached to Area teams as one possible approach towards solving problems that this study has raised. The present organisational structure of Sheffield's Social Services Department (F and CS) will be used as a framework on which to base these ideas.

Group home managers would be Area-based and their number per Area would depend on the size of population being served and the priorities of the Department. An initial estimate is for each Area to have one officer who would be directly accountable, not to the Area Officer in charge, but *jointly* to two Assistant Directors (Fieldwork and Residential/Day Services). He/she would occupy, for example, the status of a Principal Social Worker, would work at Area level maintaining close contacts with Area Team members and be assured, through liaison with the respective Area Officer, of certain fieldwork and domiciliary resources. A group home manager would fulfil two overall functions:

a. setting up and acting as manager of Area-based group homes;

b. achieving and maintaining effective liaison with a range of other officers, both internal and external to the Department for the purpose of securing residents and establishing their support in the community.

Setting up group homes requires an active liaison with the LA Housing Department for the acquisition of housing stock. Public sector housing provides a huge potential for mentally handicapped people, including those who are very dependent indeed. Most housing, particularly that built recently, has high amenity standards. An increasing proportion is built to mobility standards which make it convenient for mentally handicapped people who have a physical

153

disability to live in. Housing authorities can be asked to adapt ordinary housing to provide extra space if it is needed, or to provide a downstairs bedroom and lavatory. The range of housing provided is widening, and single person accommodation or two-person flats may suit some mentally handicapped people who do not need a great deal of support.

Many housing authorities already allow people in hospital to register on their waiting list and they may give points for medical priority. If they use their nomination rights flexibly, they can provide housing opportunities for many people now in hospital or hostels. There is scope for far greater cooperation between housing, social services and health authorities, and voluntary agencies to provide housing and the support that is needed. For instance, social services, health authorities and individual hospitals can all hold nomination rights to selected housing which enable them to house their clients outside the waiting list for housing.

Housing associations

These have a major role to play in housing mentally handicapped people. There is a growing interest among them in providing housing for people with special needs and funds are available for housing projects for people who are in need of care and support. Housing associations can work together with voluntary agencies which understand the needs of mentally handicapped people to produce schemes where an association provides the building and others provide the specialist input and support*.

Private sector housing

Statutory or voluntary agencies may prefer to buy housing on the open market (as, for example, GH1) if they feel it will provide better accommodation for their clients. This has its advantages: the choice of properties will be wider, and very specific requirements — like being near the family — can be met. Like housing association provision it also enables the integration of mentally handicapped people into ordinary community settings.

Legislation: powers and duties

Three pieces of legislation cover the powers and duties of local authorities to provide accommodation for mentally handicapped people: the National Assistance Act, 1948; the Mental Health Act, 1959; and the National Health Services Act, 1977 (Section 21). It is because the responsibility for providing accommodation under these Acts rests with

---

* Special Projects Promotion Allowance (DoE Circular 64/78) contributes to the cost of negotiating a management agreement with a specialist group. It does not cover running costs.

social services and health authorities rather than with housing departments that there has been a confusion between the need for housing and the need for care, and that the potential role of housing authorities has been neglected.

The Chronically Si⁓ led Persons Act, 1970, requires local housing auth⁓ special needs of handicapped people when t⁓ ⁓t does not exclude mentally handicapp⁓ ⁓nterpreted to cover only physically disab⁓ there has been a development of wheel⁓ ⁓pecially adapted housing. There is, howev⁓ ⁓ current housing legislation to stop housing authori⁓ from providing the full range of housing that mentally handicapped people may need. Housing authorities already have the power to provide shared and single tenancies, bedsitters, group homes, sheltered housing with a warden, lodgings and hostels.

The Housing Act, 1957 sets out the main housing functions of local authorities and their duties to consider the needs of their area and to provide accordingly. The Act also gives them the power to acquire property and land.

The Housing Act, 1969 gives the local authority the duty to carry out an inspection of its area 'from time to time' in order to see how it should be meeting its obligations under the 1957 Act.

The Housing Act, 1974 extended the 1957 Act to include hostel accommodation which provides either board or facilities for the preparation of food. The Act prescribes the role of the Housing Corporation and provides for the registration of and granting of financial help to housing associations. It also gives housing authorities power to make improvement grants to handicapped people to adapt their homes.

The Housing (Homeless Persons) Act 1977 places upon local housing authorities the duty to offer at least advice and assistance to anyone who is homeless or threatened with homelessness. Authorities are required to secure that some form of accommodation becomes available to anyone who is homeless and in 'priority need' as defined in the Act — this includes homeless people who are vulnerable as a result of old age, mental illness or handicap or physical disability.

DoE Circular 14/83: *Housing Act, 1974. Housing Corporation and Housing Associations.* DoE Circular 103/77 (Welsh Office Circular 162/77): *Housing Act, 1974. Part III. Calculation and payment of housing association grant* replaced by Housing Corporation Circular 4/83. *Housing Act 1974: Housing Association Grant: Administration allowances: April 1983–March 1984.* Housing Corporation Circular 1/77: *Joint Funding Arrangements for Caring Hostel Projects.* A later source is the Shared Housing Supplement to the Scheme Work Procedure Guide.

Housing authorities and housing associations, in short, have all the powers they need to play their part in the creation of a comprehensive, community-based residential service for mentally handicapped people. Their task, in cooperation with other relevant agencies and organisations, is to use these powers to the full.

(ii) *The selection of residents — preparation and training**

The development of group homes requires managers to devise effective working links with representatives from other residential establishments, such as LA hostels and AHA hospitals and hostels. Group home managers need to liaise actively with other units in order to ensure a steady movement of residents from such units into the group homes. They need to convince unit heads of the wide range of mentally handicapped adults who can manage in a group home with fairly limited outside support.

They need to be able to counter common prejudices that other unit heads may have regarding the type of individual disability, behaviour problem or background experience that preclude a mentally handicapped person from being a suitable group home candidate. They need, for example, to assure the unit heads that if, in the end, a particular mentally handicapped individual proves incapable of living in a group home through his incompatibility with the other residents, he will be offered a place in another group home which may be more appropriate in meeting his needs, rather than their having to resort to finding an available hospital bed for him.

In spite of the claim that a wide range of individuals are capable of managing in a group home, care needs to be taken in the choosing of particular individuals who might combine together to form a group. Such residents may already be seen to nominally comprise a group through their friendship with one another in a hospital ward or a hostel. Residents can be selected from the same unit to form a group or else be hand-picked from a number of units by the staff concerned. An important factor, which has not yet been mentioned, is that of residents' being allowed to choose for themselves whether or not they would wish to live in a specific group home, rather than their having this decision made for them.

Finally, on the question of preparing residents, some units already have training houses or flats kept aside for rehabilitation purposes and these need to be used fully with the specific aim of teaching residents domestic skills and giving them an opportunity to share work and

* D. of E. 'Housing for Mentally Ill and Mentally Handicapped People' (1983). The conclusions to this report observe the difficulties of replacing residents to obtain group harmony. A further observation is that the population for whom group homes were suitable, that is relatively able people with a long term history of institutional living, is now so reduced that those now remaining in hospital need something different.

leisure tasks. When these separate facilities are not available in a residential unit, the group home manager needs to support unit heads in preparing selected residents through emphasising the relevance of developing individual skills, interdependence and friendships within small groups of residents. The present pattern of care in Rotherham HA hostel units provides a good example of what can be achieved — here the emphasis is on providing temporary rather than permanent care and efforts are being made to prepare individuals to live together as a group outside the hostel (Firth (1980)).

(iii) *The individual programme plan*

Once admitted to a group home, each resident should have an individual programme plan.* This has a vital place and forms the basis of planning for individual residents, and ensures that those who come into contact with them regularly are together seeking the best possible services for them. It also ensures a consistency of approach: because specific objectives are set and ways of attaining these are agreed among all those who work regularly with an individual, the chances of different approaches being taken along the way are lessened. Individual programme plans encourage the participation of clients and their families, no less than professionals, in both decision-making and the achievement of objectives. And finally, by pointing up the gap between what individuals need and what is currently available, individual programme plans yield invaluable information for the planning of service developments.

An individual programme plan is essentially a written programme of intervention and action which is developed by the people who are regularly involved with an individual client. It defines a continuum of development and, after an initial assessment which tries to determine the degree of the client's development deficits outlines progressive steps which the client can take in each area of development and the supports which will be needed. The overall aim is to enable the client to keep moving towards more independent functioning; plans need to be reviewed regularly, at least once a year.

It is important for the group home manager to involve relevant outsiders in the composition and monitoring of individual programme plans, examples being the clinical psychologist, teachers and day centre instructors. The last are especially important in view of the fact that the majority of group home residents may be attending adult training centres during the day and effective liaison will enable work to be done in the development of residents' independence and social skills. Individual programme goals need to be seen within the framework of goals for the group home as a unit, but whilst effort should be made to ensure the integrity of the group home, the fulfilment of individual goals may lead

---

* Referred to as a 'life plan' in the Jay Report (see para. 93 of report).

to the movement of individuals out of the home to alternative living settings.

The overall responsibility for coordinating resources and meeting individual client needs rests with the group home manager. Individual programme plans, however, stipulate regular review and monitoring and these procedures involve the cooperation of all staff personnel concerned with the client. It follows that, whereas the overall responsibility for client development is the concern of the manager, the coordination of individual client reviews would more properly need to be undertaken by different individual staff members chosen on the basis of their knowledge of the client and their involvement with him.

(iv) *The tasks of support staff*

Any type of residential service should aim to provide a home and home-life for people who cannot find these independently, thus making it possible for people to live in a home of their own. It thus should be a home-making service, that uses two kinds of resources. The first are material — the buildings in which people live and the things they use to make them places of comfort, privacy and security. The second kind are even more important — the people who staff the service and bring to it their home-making skills. People working as home-makers should have two kinds of tasks — 'doing' and 'teaching'. They should provide the settings and things which are needed to make a home and where necessary undertake the tasks of daily living for their clients. Some of these tasks would be very personal and private, others less so, but they would all be part of what is usually taken for granted as home-life. Support staff who would work as home-makers would also help their clients provide for themselves what they would need to make a home. They would teach their clients to be more independent in the business of everyday living.

Their tasks will vary considerably over time, as the needs and dependence of clients, in different areas of their lives, keep changing. Whatever the specific tasks required, though, they will fall into one of two categories: 'teaching' and 'doing'. The first involves identifying the areas where clients lack the skills they need to be independent in everyday life and helping them to acquire these skills. These tasks include problem-solving, identifying problems, setting priorities, planning and implementing solutions, preparing materials and settings, teaching particular activities and shaping behaviour. The second kind of task involves doing things for clients which they need to be able to do but cannot yet do for themselves. With very dependent clients, staff may spend much of their time in these tasks, but they will always need to put as much emphasis as possible on teaching as well.

The essential of the support staff job is that it involves both teaching and doing tasks. Very often at the moment, different kinds of staff are recruited for the two different sorts of task. There are 'domestic' staff (Home Helps) who are doers and 'care staff' (Social Workers) who combine some doing with some teaching. Yet this distinction is not a useful one, as many clients will need to be served by staff who are doers of routine daily living tasks for them, but who are also analysing their skill-deficits, and creating learning opportunities for them.

The 'model' of using Social Workers and Home Helps can nonetheless be seen as both practicable and advantageous. Each Area has a number of Social Work teams headed by a Principal, and a much larger team of Home Helps/Home Wardens headed by an Organiser — both Social Work and Home Help teams are ultimately accountable to the Area Officer. Within each Area the potential exists for combining both types of resource to meet the needs of group home clients. An advantage of using Home Helps is that they can be provided with special training.

A recently undertaken project in Coventry involving a doubling of the Home Help service showed how specially expanded programmes of training and support had been designed to encourage Home Helps to see themselves as concerned with the overall well-being of the client. 'This (had) involved the provision of both practical and emotional support, surveillance, and an alertness to the need for further Home Help — or other health or social service — support or, indeed, for a reduction in care' (Latto, 1980). For this project Home Help recruitment had been more selective than normal and the encouragement and exploitation of particular skills amongst certain Home Helps had been recognised by a slightly higher rate of pay. Generally speaking, Home Helps are not exposed to the kind of training programmes enjoyed by other staff groups in social service departments and hence it might be argued that they can be more easily trained or adapted to carry out certain specialised tasks.

For the purpose of providing direct care support to mentally handicapped adults living in a group home, an established relationship between client and Home Help is important. Home Helps should, therefore, through training be encouraged to become more closely involved with the clients' lifestyle and to feel able to help the client in dealing with the personal and practical problems of living. The type of support Home Helps are able to provide should harmonise with that of Social Workers. It may be more appropriate that a 'team' approach is less satisfactory than that which involves only Home Helps or Social Workers. It is the job of the group home manager to make an initial assessment of the needs of a group of residents and endeavour, through discussion and liaison, to match these with the staff resources available to him.

Finally, the proposition should be stressed that every human being

has a need to relate to other people and the encouragement and maintenance of relationships among individuals of a small group are a first
step towards enabling them to relate and function on a wider social
level. The provision of residential care within the community is a first
step in normalising the lives of mentally handicapped people, especially
those who have spent time in institutions. The aim of residential care
should be to provide a home-like environment where individuals have
the potential to exercise independence and freedom of choice in their
daily living arrangements. A large scale movement of mentally handicapped people into the community will familiarise the public with them
and with the special problems that they have to face. It is hoped that this
could be a major step in changing public attitudes towards them in a
direction not only of tolerance but also of acceptance.

Both doing and teaching need to be done in the ordinary activities of
everyday life — sleeping, washing, dressing, using the toilet, eating,
going out and engaging in interesting and useful activities. These home-
making tasks fall into clusters — self-care, daily living activities, recre-
ation and leisure, and work and occupation. Support staff should be
responsible for seeing that daily routines and programmes cover each of
these clusters. It is also important that their caring role is seen as going
well beyond the confines of the home. A home-life includes regular
contact with a number of people who live outside its four walls —
neighbours, family and relatives, tradespeople and casual
acquaintances. Staff will have to ensure these contacts are made and
maintained and teach the clients to make and maintain them for
themselves.

REFERENCES

Baker, B. L., Seltzer, G. B. and Seltzer, M. M. (1977) *As Close as Possible: Community Residences for Retarded Adults*. Little, Brown & Co., Boston.

Chant, J. (1977) Group Homes, *APEX*, Vol. 5, No. 1.

Craft, M. and Evans, E. *Small Group Homes for Subnormals. Range of Provision in Denbighshire*. Social Work Today, Vol. 1, No. 9, December 1970, 41–44

Dalgleish, M. and Matthews, R. (1979) *Community Reaction to Local Buildings: Pilot Study*. (Sheffield Development Project for Mentally Handicapped People, Report 3) Mental Health Buildings Evaluation, DHSS.

Dennis, N. (1963) Who needs neighbours? *New Society* 43, July.

DES (1978) Special Educational Needs: Report of the Committee of Enquiry into the Education of Handicapped Children and Young People (Warnock Report — Cmnd 7212: HMSO).

DHSS (1971) Command 4683: Better Services for the Mentally Handicapped. London: HMSO.

DHSS (1971) Feasibility Study Report Proposing a New Pattern of Service for the Mentally Handicapped in Sheffield County Borough.

DHSS (1980) Mental Handicap: Progress, Problems and Priorities. A Review of Mental Handicap Services in England since the 1971 White Paper.

DHSS (1981) Care in the Community. A Consultative Document on Moving Resources for Care in England.

DHSS (1982) Development Team for the Mentally Handicapped. Third Report: 1979–81.

Douglas, T. (1976) *Groupwork Practice*. Tavistock, London.

Edgerton, R. B. (1967) *The Cloak of Competence*. Berkley, University of California Press.

Firth, H. (1980) Personal Communication describing Rotherham AHA Mental Handicap services.

Garland, J. A. and Kolodny, R. L. (1970) Characteristics and Resolution of Scapegoating. In S. Bernstein (ed.) *Further Exploration in Groupwork*. Boston University, School of Social work.

Gardham, J. *et al* (1977) *Community Care for the Mentally Handicapped. Minimum Support Homes in Humberside*. Social Work Service No. 14.

Grunewald, K. and Thor, V. (1978) *Group Homes for Mentally Retarded Adults*, unpublished paper.

Guy's Health District, Development Group for Services for Mentally Handicapped People (1981) *Report to the District Management Team*.

Heginbotham, C. (1981) *Housing Projects for Mentally Handicapped People* CEH (Centre on Environment for the Handicapped).

Heron, A. and Phillips, J. (1977) The Sheffield Development Project on Services for the Mentally Handicapped: Implementation of the Feasibility Study Recommendations. *ERG Reports*, No. 1. Sheffield: Evaluation Research Group, Department of Psychology, The University.

Jay, P. (Chairman) (1979a) *Report of the Committee of Enquiry into Mental Handicap Nursing and Care. Volume I.* (Cmnd 7468–I) London: HMSO.

Jay, P. (Chairman) (1979b) *Report of the Committee of Enquiry into Mental Handicap Nursing and Care. Volume II: OPCS Survey of Nurses and Residential Care Staff.* (Cmnd 7468–II).

Johnson, M. (1975) *Sheltered Housing Scheme — A Report for Northgate Hospital* Adult Care Training Scheme.

King, R., Raynes, N. and Tizard, J. (1971) *Patterns of Residential Care: Sociological Studies in Institutions for Handicapped Children.* London: Routledge and Kegan Paul.

Kings Fund Project Paper No. 24 (1980) *An Oridinary Life (comprehensive locally-based residential services for mentally handicapped people).* Kings Fund Centre.

Latto, S. Help Begins at Home. *Community Care*, 24 April 1980.

Lippitt, G. L. and Seashore, E. W. (1970) The Leader looks at Group Effectiveness. (Pamphlet).

Locker, D., Rao, B. and Weddell, J. M. (1979) Knowledge of and attitudes towards mental handicap: their implications for community care. *Community Medicine*, 1(2), 127–136.

Lundblad, E. and Viktor, E. (1975) 'It's not easy to make oneself confident'. How the mentally retarded experience their situation in integrated group homes, (in Swedish). Project Mental Retardation, Ulleraker Hospital, S-750 17 Uppsala.

Malin, N. and Race, D. (1977) Voluntary Services for the Mentally Handicapped, *ERG Reports*, No. 3. Sheffield: Evaluation Research Group, Department of Psychology, The University.

Malin, N. (1982) Living Together. *Community Care*, 11 February.

Mann, P. (1965) *An Approach to Urban Sociology.* Routledge and Kegan Paul.

Mayers, J. and Timms, N. (1970) *The Client Speaks — Working Class Impressions of Casework.* Routledge and Kegan Paul.

National Development Group for the Mentally Handicapped (1980) *Improving the Quality of Services for Mentally Handicapped People.* A Checklist of Standards. DHSS.

Newcastle City Council/Newcastle AHA (Teaching) (1981) *Mentally handicapped people and their families. A Blueprint for Local Service.*

Nihara, K. (1969) Factorial Dimensions of Adaptive Behaviour in Adult Retardates. *American Journal of Mental Deficiency*, 73, No. 6.

Nihara, K. *et al* (1974) Adaptive Behaviour Scale (1974 revision) Washington DC: AAMD.

Northen, H. (1969) *Social Work with Groups*. Boulder, Col.: Columbia University Press.

Pahl, R. (1970) *Patterns of Urban Life*. Longmans.

Pushkin, R. (1976) Community confusion over abnormality needs a remedy. *Health and Social Service Journal*, 86, 1856–1857.

Race, D. G. and Race, D. M. (1979) *The 'Cherries' group home*. HMSO.

Redl, F. (1942) Group Emotion and Leadership. *Psychiatry*, 5 (4).

Royal Society for Mentally Handicapped Children and Adults (1982) *The Mencap Homes Foundation: A Plan for Development of Residential services for Mentally Handicapped People*.

Sheffield AHA (Teaching) and Sheffield Metropolitan District Council (1981) *Report of Working Party of Joint Consultative Committee convened to consider the Strategic Planning of Services for the Mentally Handicapped*.

Sigelmann, C. K. (1976) A Machiavelli for Planners: Community Attitudes and Selection of a Group Home Site. *Mental Retardation*, 14, 26–29.

Tyne, A. (1978) *'Looking at Life' — in Hospitals, Hostels, Homes and 'Units' for Adults who are Mentally Handicapped*. (Enquiry Paper 7), Campaign for the Mentally Handicapped, London.

Verba, S. (1961) Leadership: Affective and Instrumental. In *Small Groups and Political Behaviour*. Princeton, NJ, Princeton University Press.

Weber, D. E. (1978) Neighbourhood Entry in Group Home Development. *Child Welfare*, 57, 627–642, December.

Willmott, P. (1962) Housing Density and Town Design in a New Town. Town Planning Review, 33.

Zadik, T. (1980) Checklist on Measuring Abilities for Group Home Residents. Nottingham Education Department.

Appendix A

Results of A-B Scale application, comparing a sample of residents from LA hostels with all residents from LA group homes

The presentation that follows uses a similar format to that employed in the first survey (*ERG Reports*, No. 4) in that the scores are set under either three or four specifically headed divisions. This enables a broad comparison of scores for residents in the two types of unit.

(i) *Results (Part I)*:

The tables below compare the residents' performance on the tasks as headed (note that for all scores the higher the score the 'better' is the individual in terms of social competence). In these tables entries record the number of residents from each type of unit whose score falls in the appropriate range.

Independent Functioning

	0–35	36–70	71–107
LA Hostels	0	4	21
Group Homes	0	0	24

Physical Development

	0–8	9–16	17–24
LA Hostels	0	5	20
Group Homes	0	0	24

Economic Activity

	0	1–6	7–12	13–19
LA Hostels	1	6	10	8
Group Homes	0	2	5	17

Language Development

	0	1–13	14–26	27–39
LA Hostels	0	2	11	12
Group Homes	0	0	5	19

Numbers and Time

	0	1–4	5–8	9–12
LA Hostels	0	6	6	13
Group Homes	0	2	2	20

Domestic Activity

	0	1–6	7–12	13–18
LA Hostels	0	3	11	11
Group Homes	0	0	4	20

	Vocational Activity			
	0	*1–4*	*5–8*	*9–11*
LA Hostels	1	1	5	18
Group Homes	0	0	4	20

	Self-Direction			
	0	*1–7*	*8–14*	*15–20*
LA Hostels	0	1	4	20
Group Homes	0	0	7	17

	Responsibility			
	0	*1–2*	*3–4*	*5–6*
LA Hostels	0	1	13	11
Group Homes	0	0	10	14

	Socialisation			
	0	*1–9*	*10–18*	*19–26*
LA Hostels	0	0	11	14
Group Homes	0	0	8	16

In all but one of the above domains (*i.e.* Self-Direction) the group homes scores were higher. This means that overall the residents of the Sheffield group homes were rated as being more competent than the residents of the Local Authority hostels in the sets of skills contained within these domains. Marked differences occurred in Economic Activity, Language Development, Numbers and Time and Domestic Activity. These results not only correspond with those found in the first sample survey but also emphasise more strongly the differences found in that survey.

(i) *Results (Part II)*:

As stated in presenting the results of the sample survey, Part II consists of domains describing various aspects of 'undesirable behaviour'. (In these scores, note that high scores are 'bad', *i.e.* the reverse of Part I).

	Violent and Destructive Behaviour			
	0	*1–10*	*11–20*	*21+*
LA Hostels	12	13	—	—
Group Homes	16	8	—	—

	Anti-social Behaviour			
	0	*1–10*	*11–20*	*21+*
LA Hostels	8	14	1	2
Group Homes	4	17	2	1

	Rebellious Behaviour			
	0	*1–10*	*11–20*	*21+*
LA Hostels	11	13	—	1
Group Homes	6	17	1	—

Untrustworthy Behaviour

	0	1–5	6–10	10+
LA Hostels	16	8	1	1
Group Homes	9	13	1	1

Withdrawal

	0	1–5	6–10	10+
LA Hostels	13	8	4	—
Group Homes	8	13	2	1

Stereotyped Behaviours

	0	1–5	6–10	10+
LA Hostels	20	5	—	—
Group Homes	19	5	—	—

Inappropriate Interpersonal Manners

	0	1–5	6+
LA Hostels	16	5	4
Group Homes	19	5	—

Unacceptable Vocal Habits

	0	1–5	6+
LA Hostels	13	11	1
Group Homes	11	13	—

Unacceptable or Eccentric Habits

	0	1–10	11–20	21+
LA Hostels	13	11	1	—
Group Homes	13	11	—	—

Self-Abusive Behaviour

	0	1–5	6+
LA Hostels	23	2	—
Group Homes	22	2	—

Hyperactive Tendencies

	0	1–5	6+
LA Hostels	20	5	—
Group Homes	15	9	—

Sexually Aberrant Behaviour

	0	1–10	11+
LA Hostels	12	12	1
Group Homes	18	6	1

Psychological Disturbances

	0	1–10	11–20	21+
LA Hostels	5	17	2	1
Group Homes	1	19	3	1

	Medication		
	0	1–5	6+
LA Hostels	19	6	—
Group Homes	15	9	1

The above scores do not indicate any major differences between the residents of group homes and Local Authority hostels, as in most cases they are very similar. In fact, on balance, the 'hostel group' has a slight edge over the group home one in that seven of the fourteen domains show the hostels with a slightly better score. On the whole, however, it can be said that there are few residents in either type of unit with serious behaviour problems. In assessing the importance of behaviour problems for enabling successful group home living, these results indicate possibilities for the extension of group home care to residents in the hostel sector.

(ii) *Individual domains*:

This section presents examples of the scores of group home residents taken from the above assessment on particular domains of the A-B Scale. The basis of selection was, for Part I of the Scale, in respect of domains where clear differences in scoring emerged between group home and hostel residents, and for Part II, in respect of those where group home scores were particularly high.

Part I

A. *Economic Activity*

Over twice the number of group home as opposed to hostel residents had scores in the highest division. This domain includes two sub-domains entitled respectively — A. Money Handling and Budgeting and B. Shopping Skills. To look at the first of these:

Money Handling (Circle only *ONE*)	
Uses bank facilities in community	6
Understand fully banking facilities in hospital	5
Can give change of £1	4
Adds coins (50p, 10p, 5p, 2p, 1p) up to 68p	3
Uses money but does not know what change to expect	2
Realises money has value, but does not use money	1
Has no idea of the value of money	0

Seven out of twenty-four group home residents scored top marks on this, four of whom came from the same home. It is not possible to draw firm conclusions relating to the *abilities* of residents to carry out this task as much is dependent on the opportunities offered to them by support workers. However it can be said that an ability to use bank facilities in the community is an indication of sophistication not normally associated with the individuals labelled mentally handicapped which casts doubts on standard classification criteria in use.

Budgeting (Check *ALL* statements which apply)	
Saves money or tokens for a particular purpose	—
Budgets fares, meals etc.	—

167

Spends money with some planning	—
Controls own major expenditures	—
None of the above	—

Eight out of twenty-four group home residents scored on all four of these items, six from two homes (GH1 and 3). These skills are concerned with finance management and obviously, a person who is able to score on all of them is capable of managing an income both sensibly and responsibly. Taken together these two sections, Money Handling and Budgeting, show some expected degree of overlap at the high score end of the range: six out of eight residents in two group homes (GH1 and 4) have high scores in both these sections. Ten residents score for 'controls own major expenditures', four of whom live together in one of the homes (GH3). At the low end of the score range, four residents scored nil, two of whom had scored the same in the aforementioned section. The other two who both had relatively high scores in 'Money Handling' belonged to the same home (GH5).

The other sub-domain is entitled Shopping Skills and again is broken into two sections:

Errands (Circle only *ONE*)

Goes to several shops and specifies different items	4
Goes to one shop and specifies one item	3
Goes on local errands for simple purchasing without a note	2
Goes on local errands for simple purchasing with a note	1
Cannot be sent on errands	0

On reading the above items it would seem that their order of priority is not clear. For example, should the second listed item score higher than the third? For it to do so 'Goes to one shop and specifies one item' should be interpreted as an ability to seek out an appropriate shop for buying a named item which can be asked for and described in an accurate way, and 'Goes on local errands for simple purchasing without a note' should be interpreted as an ability to visit local (and hence familiar) shops and request simple items, where no additional explanation or information is needed. The Manual on the Adaptive Behaviour Scale instrument does not advice on this and although the present writer is suggesting this interpretation, it does not follow that it was used by staff members completing the assessments. As for the results on this section, the general level of scoring was very high: all but two group home residents scored either 3 or 4. The low scorers are the same individuals who scored low in the previous sub-domain.

Purchasing (Circle only *ONE*)

Buys all own clothing	5	5
Buys own clothing accessories	4	4
Makes minor purchases without help (sweets, soft drinks etc)	3	3
Does shopping with slight supervision		2
Does shopping with close supervision		1
Does no shopping		0

This relates to the previous section as it involved shopping skills in the broad sense; hence one would expect a similarity in the results: all but three residents scored either 4 or 5. The two consistently low scoring residents were both rated as 'does shopping with close supervision'.

B. *Language Development*

The sub-domains are labelled respectively. A. Expression, B. Comprehension, and C. Social Language Development and comprise the following:

Writing (Circle only *ONE*)

Writes sensible and understandable letters	5
Writes short notes and memos	4
Writes or prints forty words	3
Writes or prints ten words	2
Writes or prints own name	1
Cannot write or print any words	0

Overall scores in this section were not high: ten residents had scores of four and above whereas the remainder showed little evidence of writing skills. Note that in each of the larger group homes (with 5 residents) there was at least one resident who could 'write sensible and understandable letters'. Seven residents could only write or print their own name and five could not write or print any words. The writing skills of residents in two homes (GH4 and 6) were very few indeed: no one at GH4 scored more than 2 and the resident at GH6 scored 0.

Preverbal Expression (Check *ALL* statements which apply)

Nods head or smiles to express happiness	—
Indicates hunger	—
Indicates wants by pointing or vocal noises	—
Chuckles or laughs when happy	—
Expresses pleasure or anger by vocal noises	—
Is able at least to say a few words	—
None of the above	—

All 24 residents scored for each of the above position items.

Articulation (Check *ALL* statements which apply — if no speech, check 'NONE' and enter '0' in the circle)

Speech is low, weak, whispered or difficult to hear	—
Speech is slow, deliberate or laboured	—
Speech is hurried, accelerated or pushed	—
Speaks with blocking, halting or other irregular interruptions	—
None of the above	—

Two-thirds of the group had no problem in this section, whilst a further six scored on any one of the items — usually the last one, and two scored on two of the items. A similar high scoring pattern appeared on the two final sections of this sub-domain, with the same four residents having failed to score top marks on both.

169

Sentences (Circle only *ONE*)
Sometimes uses complex sentences containing 'because', 'but', etc.   3
Asks questions using words such as 'why', 'how', 'what', etc.   2
Speaks in simple sentences   1
Speaks in primitive phrases only, or is non-verbal   0
Word Usage (Circle only *ONE*)
Talks about action when describing pictures   4
Names people or objects when describing pictures   3
Names familiar objects   2
Asks for things by their appropriate names   1
Is non-verbal or nearly non-verbal   0

The second sub-domain contained two sections: Reading and Complex Instructions.

Reading (Circle only *ONE*)
Reads book suitable for children nine years or older   5
Reads books suitable for children seven years old   4
Reads simple stories or comics   3
Reads various signs, e.g. 'NO PARKING', 'ONE WAY', 'MEN',' 'WOMEN', etc.   2
Recognises fewer than ten words or none at all   0

Ten residents had basic reading skills, *i.e.* scoring three or above. There were three of these high scoring residents in each of three homes (GH1, 2 and 3) being usually the same individuals who had high scores on writing skills. Nine residents scored nil in this section, meaning that they were only able to recognise 'fewer than ten words or none at all'. Two further findings were noticeable: the first was that all but one resident in one of the larger homes (GH5) were illiterate, and the second was that in two homes (GH4 and 6) none of the residents had literary skills. All residents scored full marks on the following section:

Complex Instructions (Check *ALL* statements which apply)
Understands instructions containing prepositions,
e.g. 'on', 'in', 'behind', 'under', etc.   —
Understands instructions referring to the order in which things must be done,
e.g. 'first do, then do'   —
Understands instructions requiring a decision:
'if----, do this, but if not, do----'   —
None of the above   —

The last-domain, Social Language Development, covered conversation, and other related aspects of language development. On the first all residents scored full marks.

Conversation (Check *ALL* statements which apply)
Uses phrases such as 'please' and 'thank you'   —
Is sociable and talks during meals   —
Talks to others about sports, family, group activities, etc.   —
None of the above   —

Miscellaneous Language Development (Check *ALL* statements which apply)

Can be reasoned with —
Obviously responds when talked to —
Talks sensibly —
Reads books, newspapers, magazines for enjoyment —
Repeats a story with little or no difficulty —
Fills in the main items on application form reasonably well —
None of the above —

All but two residents scored for the first three items in the above section. 19 out of the group were rated as being able to 'repeat a story with little or no difficulty'; only two scored on the last item, both of them from GH3. Taking this domain as a whole, high scores had been apparent throughout in areas relating to the ability to express and comprehend, whereas there was considerable variation of scoring in reading and writing skills.

C. *Numbers and Time*

Numbers (Circle only *ONE*)

Does simple addition and subtraction   5
Counts ten or more objects   4
Mechanically counts to ten   3
Counts two objects by saying 'one....two....'   2
Discriminates between 'one' and 'many' or 'a lot'   1
Has no understanding of numbers   0

Half of the group scored five in the above section which was high when considered in the context of what it actually meant for individuals classified as mentally handicapped to be able to do addition and subtraction sums. No resident scored nil showing that the remainder had at least some basic perception of numeracy.

Time (Check *ALL* statements which apply)

Tells time by clock or watch correctly to the minute —
Understands time intervals, e.g. between '3.30 and 4.30' —
Understands time equivalents, e.g. '9.15 is the same as 'quarter past nine' —
Associates time on clock with various actions and events —
None of the above —

17 out of 24 residents scored on each of these items. The remainder varied, none of whom managed to score on the first item. All but three of these scored on the last item which could have been classed as the 'easiest' of the four skills as it constituted a basic ability to relate daytime events to clock times. Two residents scored nil on this section which was consistent with their earlier poor scoring record on other skills requiring some measure of concentrated learning e.g. use of money, writing. All but one of the group scored full marks on the following section:

Time Concept (Check *ALL* statements which apply)

Name the days of the week —
Refers correctly to 'morning' and 'afternoon' —

Understands difference between day-week, minute-hour, month-year, etc. —
None of the above —

D. *Domestic Ability*

The domain was divided into three parts namely Cleaning, Kitchen and Other Domestic Activities. The first was sub-divided into Room Cleaning and Laundry:

Room Cleaning (Circle only *ONE*)
Cleans room well, e.g. sweeping, dusting, tidying   2
Cleans room but not thoroughly   1
Does not clean room at all   0

15 residents scored on the highest of these items with all but one of the remainder scoring on the second item. With regard to Laundry, again the scores were high but then there was a high level of interrelatedness among the items:

Laundry (Check *ALL* statements which apply)
Washes clothing   —
Dries clothing   —
Folds clothing   —
Irons clothing when appropriate   —
None of the above   —

18 out of the total group scored on each one of these items, including only one of the males. The male (married) resident in GH2 scored nil as he was rated as 'having no opportunity' to perform these tasks.

The next sub-domain, Kitchen, covered table setting, food preparation and table clearing. As in the case of other items on this domain, scoring may have reflected opportunity to practice skills rather than actual levels of ability. On 'table setting' residents either scored three or two.

Table Setting (Circle only *ONE*)
Places all eating utensils, as well as napkins salt and pepper, sugar, etc. in positions learned   3
Places plates, glasses and utensils in positions learned   2
Places silver, plates, cups, etc. on the table   1
Does not set table at all   0

Food Preparation (Circle only *ONE*)
Prepares an adequate complete meal (may use canned or frozen food)   3
Mixes and cooks simple food, e.g. fries eggs, makes pancakes, cooks TV dinners   2
Prepares simple foods requiring no mixing or cooking, e.g. sandwiches, cold cereal, etc.   1
Does not prepare food at all   0

On the above, eight residents were able to 'prepare an adequate complete meal'. Only one home — GH6 — did not have someone who was able to do this. The majority of the remainder were rated as being able to 'cook simple food' and no one scored nil.

Table Clearing (Circle only *ONE*)

Clears table of breakfast dishes and glassware	2
Clears table of unbreakable dishes and silverware	1
Does not clear table at all	0

All but one resident scored two on the above section. The final sub-domain was as follows:

General Domestic Activity (Check *ALL* statements which apply)

Washes dishes well	—
Makes beds neatly	—
Helps in household chores when asked	—
Does household tasks routinely	—
None of the above	—

20 out of the total group scored on each of the items. Three of the others scored on the third but not on the fourth item. Two residents failed to score on the first two items.

Part II

Half or more of the total population of group home residents had scores on one or more items of the following five sub-domains taken from Part II of the Scale. Individual resident scores are presented, using small alphabetical letters to identify the extent of individual resident 'maladaptive' behaviour.

		Occasionally	Frequently
A.	*Teases or Gossips about Others*		
	Gossips about others	GH1c, d, e	GH1b
		GH2a, c, d, e	GH2b
		GH5c, d	GH5a
	Tells untrue or exaggerated stories	GH1b	GH2b
	about others	GH2a, c, d, e	GH5a
		GH4a	
	Teases others	GH2a, d	GH2b
	Picks on others	GH5a, d	GH1b
		GH3c	
	Makes fun of others	GH2a, b	—
	Other (specify:)		
	None of the above		
B.	*Resists Following Instructions,*	Occasionally	Frequently
	Requests or Orders		
	Gets upset if given a direct order	GH2a, b	—
	Plays deaf and does not follow	GH1b, 2a,	GH2b
	instructions	GH3a, c	
		GH5b,	
		GH6a	
	Does not pay attention to instructions	GH1e, GH3a	—
		GH5b	

Refuses to work on assigned subject	GH3a, GH5b	—
Hesitates for long periods before doing assigned tasks	GH2, GH3a,c,e GH5a, c	GH2e
Does the opposite of what was requested	—	—
Other (specify:)		
None of the above		

C. *Lies or Cheats*

	Occasionally	Frequently
Twists the truth to own advantage	GH1b GH2b,c,d,e GH4a GH5b, d GH6a	GH2a GH5a
Cheats in games, tests, assignments etc.	—	—
Lies about situations	GH1b GH2b, d GH5b	GH2a GH5a
Lies about self	GH2, GH3a, GH5b	GH2a
Lies about others	GH2b, GH3a, GH5b, GH6a	GH2a
Other (specify:)		
None of the above		

D. *Reacts Poorly to Criticism*

	Occasionally	Frequently
Does not talk when corrected	GH1a, c, d GH2a, GH3a GH5e	GH1e GH5a
Withdraws or pouts when criticised	GH2a GH3b, e GH5b	GH1c, d, e
Becomes upset when criticised	GH1a,b,c,d,e GH2b GH3a,b,c,d,e	GH2a GH5b, c, e
Screams and cries when corrected	—	—
Other (specify:)		
None of the above		

E. *Reacts Poorly to Frustration*

	Occasionally	Frequently
Blames own mistakes on others	GH2a, b, e GH3a, b, c	GH1b GH5a, b, d GH6a
Withdraws or pouts when thwarted	GH1e, GH2d GH3a, b GH6a	GH2a, b, e
Becomes upset when thwarted	GH2a, e GH3a, e	GH2b GH5a, b

174

	GH5a, d, e	
	GH6a	
Throws temper tantrums when does	GH2e	GH2b
not get own way	GH3c	GH5b
	GH6a	

Other (specify:)
None of the above

Appendix B

Interview Schedule: Group home residents

A. Basic Details

1. Date _____
2. Code no. of interviewee _____
3. Name _____
4. Date of Birth _____
5. Accommodation, address _____
6. Work _____
7. Marital status _____
8. Children _____

B. Support from relatives

1. What relatives do you have? ....

2. Which relatives do you see (S) or hear from (H)? ....

3. How often do you see (S) or hear from (H) them? ....

4. When did you last see _____? ....

5. When was the time before that? ....

6. What do you do when you see them? ....

7. What help do you get from relatives? ....

   Money help (includes borrowing) ....

   Gifts? ....   How? ....

8. Do you help them?   How? ....

	Person 1	Person 2	Person 3	Person 4	Person 5	Person 6
	S					
	H					
	S					
	H					

C. Support from neighbours

	Person 1	Person 2	Person 3	Person 4	Person 5	Person 6

1. Which neighbours do you know? ....

   | Strongly like |
   | Quite like |
   | Indifferent |
   | Quite dislike |
   | Strongly dislike |

2. What do you think of them? ....

3. How often do you see them? ....

4. When did you last see _____ ?

5. When was the time before that ....

6. How often do you talk to them? ....

7. When did you last talk to _____ ?

8. When was the time before that? ....

9. For how long do you talk to them? ....

10. What do you talk about? ....

11. What help do you get from them? ....

    Money help (includes borrowing)? ....

    Gifts? ....

12. Do you help them?   How? ....

D. Support from friends (1) and (2)

	Person 1	Person 2	Person 3	Person 4	Person 5	Person 6
1. What friends have you? Do you have a special friend? ..... Mark (S)						
2. What do they do for a living?						
3. Where do they live?						
Strongly like						
Quite like						
Indifferent						
4. What do you think of them?						
5. How often do you see them?						
6. How often do you talk to them (include both phone conversations and personal confrontations)						
7. For how long do you talk to them? (as above)						
8. What do you talk about?						
9. What else do you do with them?						
10. What help do you get from them? .... Money help (includes borrowing)? .... Gifts?						
11. Do you help them? How?						

178

E. Support from Social Services agencies

1. What cash benefits do you get regularly? Such as any of the following? ....

Unemploy-ment	Sickness	Social Security	Other

2. Do any of the following visit you? ....

Social Worker(1)	Social Worker(2)	Welfare Assistant	Home Help(1)	Home Help(2)	A.T.C. Staff	Doctor	Hospital person 1	Hospital person 2	Other

3. When and how often? ....

	Social Worker(1)	Social Worker(2)	Welfare Assistant	Home Help(1)	Home Help(2)	A.T.C. Staff	Doctor	Hospital person 1	Hospital person 2	Other
Strongly like										
Quite like										
Indifferent										
Quite dislike										
Strongly dislike										

4. What do you think of them?

	Social Worker(1)	Social Worker(2)	Welfare Assistant	Home Help(1)	Home Help(2)	A.T.C. Staff	Doctor	Hospital person 1	Hospital person 2	Other
Practical jobs										
Fixing Arrangements										
Money matters										

5. What help do you get from these people? (who visit)

	Social Worker(1)	Social Worker(2)	Welfare Assistant	Home Help(1)	Home Help(2)	A.T.C. Staff	Doctor	Hospital person 1	Hospital person 2	Other
Gifts										
Advice										
Friendship										
Other										

	Social Worker	A.T.C. person	Hospital person	Doctor	Other	Other	Other
Practical jobs							
Fixing Arrangements							
Money matters							
Gifts							
Advice							
Friendship							
Other							

6. What other people do you get help from? ....
(who don't visit)

What kind of help? ....

F. Benefactor

1. Who is the person you first turn to when you need help? ....

If this person has not been mentioned in the above please answer the following:

2. What does this person do for a living? _____

3. Where does he/she live? _____

4. How often do you see this person? _____

5. When did you last see ....? _____

6. When was the time before that? _____

7. How often do you talk to this person? _____

8. When did you last talk to.............. _____

9. When was the time before that? _____

10. For how long do you talk to him? _____

11. What do you talk about _____

12. What do you think of that person? _____

Strongly like		
Quite like		
Indifferent		

G. Leisure activities

1. How do you spend your time? ·················

2. How often do you do these thing? ·················

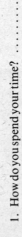

1	2	3	4

181

Appendix C

Job Description..................   Name of group home..............

Code no. of interviews.............   Date.............................

1. *Decision-making*

(a) What formal decision-making bodies exist (at any level) for the group home?

(b) Who attends each?

(c) How often do they meet?

(d) What do they make decisions on?

2. *Selection of residents*

(a) What preparation/training for independent living did the residents receive *before* moving to the home?

After moving to the home?

(b) What is the process used to select residents and who were/are involved in this process?

(c) Has this person been used for *all* those selected and have the same persons involved in the described procedure been involved every time? Are these the persons currently involved in the decisions of resident selection?

(d) What is the procedure for the introduction of new residents? Has this been the same for all new residents and if not can you describe the differences in procedure that have occurred?

3. *Treatment of residents*

(a) Who decides on how and where they are to be employed during the working day?

(b) Is the progress of individual residents monitored? If so, by whom/how?

4. *Staffing Support*

(a) How are decisions reached about (i) the staff support required for each home and (ii) the actual selection and appointment of such staff?

(b) Is the carrying out of support staff duties monitored? If so, by whom/how?

(c) Have there been any changes in staffing personnel since the home opened? If so, what?

5. *Finances of residents*

(a) Who deals with these?

(b) What is the procedure? (Breakdown of separate monies needed).

(c) If any changes have been found necessary in this procedure, please indicate their nature, the reasons for them and when they occurred.

6. *Social/recreational activities of residents*

(a) Is there a policy for providing such activities? If so, could you describe what it is?

(b) Does anyone take responsibility for providing these? If so, who?

(c) What has been/is provided?

(d) What is your personal opinion as to whether support services should take responsibility for this?

7. *Maintenance/equipment*

(a) Who decides on repairs and maintenance in the home?
Who decides on equipment items in the home — type and quantity?

(b) What is the procedure for obtaining equipment items and repairs/maintenance?

(c) How effective is it?
Illustrate by example.

8. *Transfer of residents*

(a) On what grounds would a resident (i) be removed from the home or (ii) be considered ready for transfer on from the home?

(b) Could you describe (i) how decisions of this kind have been reached, (ii) who has been involved in the making of these decisions and (iii) whether and how the procedure has been changed during the history of the home.

9. *Staff role and objectives*

(a) Describe the kind of residents that you are serving.

(b) What are you trying to do for them?

(c) How are you trying to do this?

(d) Describe the kind of residents you think the home should serve (if different).

(e) What would you do if you had the residents you think this home should serve (if not those who are there now)?

(f) How would you go about this?

(g) Do you think that this should be their permanent residence or should they eventually move on elsewhere?

(h) For whom do you think group homes should be provided?
Why?

(i) Were you provided with any inservice/specialised training for this job?
If so, what?

(j) What is your position vis a vis the larger organisation in which you work? (Diagram if necessary).

(k) What is the chain of accountability starting from the group home?

10. *Legal status*

What is the legal status of both the residents and the home?

Printed in the UK for HMSO
Dd.736779 C10 9/83